Armour at War

The First Cruisers

The origin, design, development, production and operational use of the British A9 Cruiser Tank Mk. I and A10 Cruiser Tank Mk. II

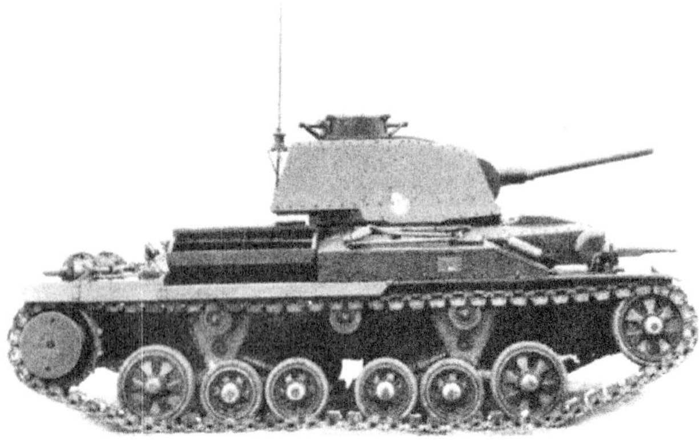

Contents

Contents

Images used in this book 5
The Armour at War Series 7
Introduction 11
Historical Context 15
Origin 25
Design 33
    The A9 33
    The A10 49
    Variants 54
        A10 Cruiser Tank Mk. IIA 54
        Close Support (CS) Version 54
        A9s and A10s in North Africa 55
        Experimental Bridgelayer 55
Production and Operational Deployment 57
    A9 Production 57
    A10 Production 59
    Operational Deployment 61
        France 61
        North Africa 66
        Greece 68
Enemies and Allies 69
    Germany 69
    Italy 76

  France 82
In Combat 87
  France 87
  North Africa 104
  Greece...119
Colour Schemes and Markings..................................123
  Colour Schemes 123
    France 127
    The Middle East 129
    Greece..132
  Markings 134
Surviving Examples 139
Conclusion 145
Further Reading 149
Other Books in the *Armour at War* Series 153
About the Author..155

Images used in this book

The images included in this book come from two main sources: The British Imperial War Museum and the German Federal Archives, Deutsches Bundesarchiv.

A large number of wartime images have been released by the Imperial War Museum on the IWM Non-Commercial Licence. Photographs taken by a member of the armed forces during their active service duties are covered by Crown Copyright which is considered expired 50 years after their creation and these images are now in the public domain.

The Bundesarchiv has also placed a large number of images taken by wartime German military photographers in the public domain.

All the images used in this book are in the public domain.

Copyright © Steve MacGregor 2021 - All rights reserved

No part of this book or any portion thereof may be reproduced or transmitted in any form or by any means, electronic or mechanical, including photocopying, recording, or by any information storage and retrieval system without the written permission of the publisher, except where permitted by applicable law.

The Armour at War Series

Given the sheer volume of books, articles and websites devoted to the military hardware of World War Two, you might wonder whether we really need another series of books about the tanks of World War Two.

There are many good books looking at the strategic conduct of the war. There are great books looking at particular battles. There are excellent books looking at combat from the point of view of individuals, units and theatres. There are books about the design and development of weapon systems, and there are a few books about the political situation that led to these designs.

The purpose of this series is a little different. Each book is a longitudinal study of a particular tank or a related group of tanks. The effectiveness of any weapon system is constrained both by its features and capabilities and its ability to complete the task it was designed to undertake. In the real world, few engineers in any field sit down in front of a blank sheet of paper and attempt to create the best possible new design. Each tank design is limited by the availability of existing components that can be utilized, the experience of the use in combat of other similar designs, and of course, by financial and manufacturing issues.

To understand how a particular tank performed it's necessary to understand not just the technical aspects of its design, but what led to that design. Understanding those elements means placing any design within in the context of the prevailing political, social technological, doctrinal and economic circumstances. That's what this series is about. It traces the development of a particular tank from its origin, through its design, to its eventual deployment on the battlefield.

On the battlefield, this series look at how the men who served and fought in these tanks felt about them. Many tanks that are widely disregarded now were appreciated by those who used them on the battlefield. Many which on paper look like great designs weren't liked at all by their crews. As far as possible, this series uses quotes from the people who knew these tanks best: the soldiers who crewed them in combat.

Each book is intended not as an exhaustive guide to every single variation of a particular model of tank or as an examination of its every operational use. Instead, it seeks to explain why a tank took the form it did and to examine how successful (or unsuccessful) it was when tested in the chaos and violence of combat.

I hope you enjoy this book and the Armour at War Series.

Introduction

This book is the first of three in the Armour at War series covering all British Cruiser Tanks. The story of these tanks began in the mid-1930s when the British Army began to consider a wholly new armoured tactical doctrine. This envisaged units comprising large formations of highly mobile, well-armed tanks operating independently. There was, however, a major problem: Britain did not possess a single highly mobile, well-armed tank. Instead, the British Army had large numbers of light tanks, ideal for colonial protection but unable to fight enemy armour, and a few lumbering remnants of an earlier doctrine that required slow, heavy tanks to support infantry advances.

It was clear that an entirely new class of tank was needed. These were what came to be known as the Cruiser Tanks, agile and capable of fighting enemy armour. The design of the very first of these, the A9 Cruiser Tank Mk. I began in 1935 and the first prototype was delivered for evaluation in 1936. Concurrently, design work progressed on the more heavily armoured A10 Cruiser Tank Mk. II and the prototype of that tank was delivered in 1937. Evaluation showed that both designs had major problems. The deteriorating political situation in Europe and the prospect of a war with Nazi Germany meant that Britain had an urgent need for these new tanks and, despite their problems, both new tanks were accepted for service with only minor changes.

When the war began in September 1939, the A9 was in service with the British Army and the A10 entered service before the end of that year. When Germany invaded the West in May 1940, A9s and A10s formed the bulk of the British Cruiser force deployed against them in France. In less than four weeks of combat both types proved vulnerable in combat and both suffered from persistent reliability issues that meant that more of these tanks were lost to breakdowns than to enemy action. Most of the A9s and A10s sent to France were destroyed or abandoned there.

With the fall of France, Britain found itself standing alone against the combined military might of Nazi Germany and Fascist Italy. In North Africa in late 1940, British and Commonwealth forces faced a large-scale Italian attack. Many British armoured units in the Middle East were also equipped with A9s and

A10s but, fortunately, Italian tanks proved even less effective and the British Cruisers achieved some notable victories. In early 1941, German tanks arrived with the Afrika Korps and once again the early Cruisers proved to be less than effective in combat against German tanks and crews.

A common sight in 1940/41: An A10 Cruiser Tank k. II abandoned after shedding a track.

Image: Deutsches Bundesarchiv, Bild 101I-161-0317-26 / Bauer / CC-BY-SA 3.0 via Wikimedia Commons

When Germany launched an attack on Greece in April 1941, Britain sent an armoured force to oppose them comprising more than 50 A10 tanks. During the short and unsuccessful campaign that followed, more than

75% of the British tanks were put out of action by breakdowns and the remainder were unable to stop or even significantly slow the German advance. All the A10s sent to Greece were abandoned or destroyed there.

During the remainder of 1941, A9s and A10s continued to be used in North Africa but, faced with improved German armour, they were almost completely ineffective and by the end of that year all had been withdrawn from front-line service.

How did this come about? Why was the design of these new tanks so rushed and compromised? Why, when they had clear faults, were they accepted for service without significant modifications? Most importantly, why were British tank crews sent into action in tanks that were catastrophically unreliable and fundamentally unsuited for many of the roles in which they were used?

This is the fascinating story of the A9 Cruiser Tank Mk. I and the A10 Cruiser Tank Mk. II. It explains the historical context behind their development, why they took the form they did, why they were rushed into service and how they fared in combat. This is the story of the first Cruisers.

Historical Context

Britain and France were two of the first nations to develop and use tanks during the First World War and Britain became the world leader in tank design. When the war finally ended, Britain's Tank Corps had grown to 25 battalions. After the war ended, it was allowed to decline in size and by the time that it became the Royal Tank Corps five years later, only four battalions remained. Even as the Tank Corps was shrinking, visionaries such as Colonel J. F. C. Fuller and Basil Liddell Hart were describing a completely different concept of armoured warfare, where fleets of fast, light tanks would form the core of mobile, combined-arms formations.

In 1927 Britain created the Experimental Mechanized Force (EMF) to test these radical new theories. This was arguably the first independent mobile, combined-arms armoured formation of its kind and it included not just tanks but also mechanised infantry. It pioneered the use of radio voice communication and close co-operation with the Royal Air Force (RAF). Despite its radical nature and success in trials, the EMF was disbanded, a victim of both economic cuts and a failure to understand how such a force could fit within conventional British military doctrine.

Vickers Mk. II Medium tanks in the 1920s. The EMF included both this type and the earlier Vickers Medium Mk. I as well as light tanks.

Image: Imperial War Museum via Wikimedia Commons

The British Army was relatively small (less than 100,000 men) and focused on the protection of British colonies abroad and the defence of the British Isles. A force such as the EMF would have been a powerful and flexible fighting force in a major European war, but most British military and political leaders saw no possibility of Britain becoming involved in such a war in the foreseeable future.

Part of the reason for this was what became known as the *"ten-year rule."* First introduced after World War One, British estimates of the size of military forces required were based on the assumption that *"the British Empire would not be engaged in any great war during the next ten years."* There was little sound reasoning behind this beyond wishful thinking and a desire to avoid the carnage of another world war. Confidently predicting ten years into the future is always difficult, and in the turmoil of post-war Europe, it proved to be a dangerous illusion.

Despite this, by 1928 the *ten-year rule* had become so embedded in British political and military planning that it led to stagnation in the design and adoption of new weapons and new approaches such as the EMF. Assuming that ten years would be available to build up the army, navy and air force if those branches were required to face a new threat led to complacency. Military spending declined sharply, from £766 million in 1920 to £102 million in 1932.

The bulk of the remaining military budget went to Royal Navy, with whatever remained being spent on developments for the army and air force. The leisurely pace of developments is illustrated by the gestation of what was intended to be a significant new British heavy tank: the A1 Independent.

The story of the A1 began in late 1922 when the General Staff of the British Army produced a specification for a new heavy tank with improved trench crossing ability. The only British company capable of designing such a tank, the engineering conglomerate Vickers Limited, submitted a design proposal in response to this specification.

The Vickers A1E1 Independent prototype.

Image: Imperial War Museum via Wikimedia Commons

The design was finalized in 1925 and a prototype was delivered the following year as the A1E1 Independent.

The new tank was massive, weighing more than 30 tons, powered by a 35-litre engine and featuring no less than five turrets and an eight-man crew. The main turret was armed with a QF 3-Pounder (47mm) main gun and four auxiliary turrets each mounted a single Vickers machine gun: one could even be elevated to provide anti-aircraft defence. This was a radical departure from existing tank design and a great deal of time and effort was put into understanding how such a tank could be best used.

Vickers and the War Office tinkered with the design until 1933 when the project was abruptly cancelled after the production of only a single prototype. The main reason for the cancellation was the high cost of producing such a large, technically advanced tank. Ten years of design and development were written-off as a single stroke.

Despite the cancellation of the project, the A1E1 proved to be an influential design. In 1933 a British Army Officer, Norman Baillie-Stewart, was court-martialled for selling military secrets, including the plans for the A1E1, to German military intelligence. The German *Neubaufahrzeug*, a multi-turreted tank, was clearly influenced by the A1E1. Like the British design, the *Neubaufahrzeug* never went beyond the prototype stage.

The Russian T-35.

Image: Public Domain via Wikimedia Commons

In the early 1930s, Germany was sharing information with Russia and it seems that the plans for the A1E1 were passed on. The giant Russian T-35, introduced in 1935, was clearly based on the design of the Vickers A1E1. Although it was not used in large numbers, the T-35 was still in Russian service during the German invasion in 1941.

The influence of the A1E1, and in particular the notion of providing tanks with multiple machine gun turrets and mounts for self-defence, would persist for some time. The American M2 Medium Tank, for example, produced in limited numbers in 1940, was provided with up to nine Browning machine guns including two mounted in sponsons on the hull sides.

With the cancellation of the A1E1, the British Army focused on the procurement of existing light tanks and tankettes, mainly produced by Vickers. These had the benefit of being cheap and they were eminently suitable for defending far-flung corners of the British Empire from attack by local people armed with nothing more lethal than rifles. There was discussion of adopting a new medium tank, the A6 Medium Mk III, also designed and produced by Vickers. Only three were built and delivered to the army for testing. The cost of the new tank plus doubts about the need for such a vehicle meant that it never entered large-scale production.

It was concern about the Royal Navy that finally led to the abandonment of the *ten-year rule.* The First Sea Lord, Sir Frederick Field, submitted an alarming report to the Committee of Imperial Defence in 1931 claiming that the decline in the strength of the Navy had reached the point where it could no longer protect

Britain's colonies abroad or even assure trade with the British Isles.

The Vickers Medium Mark III. Here one of the prototypes is being used as a command tank.

Image: Imperial War Museum via Wikimedia Commons

The ten-year rule was formally dropped in 1932, but with the corollary that *"this must not be taken to justify an expanding expenditure by the Defence Services without regard to the very serious financial and economic situation."* Britain, like almost every other country in the world, was trying to deal with the Great Depression, and there simply wasn't money to spare for military expenditure.

It wasn't until threatening developments in Europe in 1935 and 1936 that consideration was finally given to expanding and modernising the British Army. Hitler and the Nazis had come to power in Germany in 1933, and it quickly became apparent that the new regime had expansionist aims. In 1935, Hitler had renounced the terms of the Treaty of Versailles that limited the German army to 100,000 men and forbade it tanks or military aircraft.

The same year, Germany reintroduced conscription and in 1936, German troops reoccupied the demilitarized Rhineland. This demilitarized zone was also a feature of the Treaty of Versailles and a vital means of preventing German aggression. But when German troops marched in, neither Britain nor France had military units capable of undertaking an effective response. It was clear that this was only the first step in achieving Hitler's ambitions in Europe and in Britain and it caused a fundamental reappraisal of the capabilities of the British Army.

One aspect of that was consideration of the role of tanks. The light tanks suitable for colonial defence would clearly not be suitable for fighting a re-equipped and aggressive Germany in Europe. The

EMF had also demonstrated the need for faster, more mobile tanks. The Vickers Mk. I and Mk. II tanks used in the EMF were relatively slow, with a top speed of less than 15mph on good ground and much less on rough going. The British Army needed new fast tanks, but although the government was coming to understand the need for rearmament, its strategic priority remained the defence of the British Isles. That meant that most of the available funds were used to upgrade the RAF, the Royal Navy and anti-aircraft defences. If it was to develop new tanks, the British Army would have to do so while spending as little money as possible.

Origin

British tank doctrine following World War One identified three types of tank according to their overall weight. Light tanks, generally from three to six tons, were relatively fast but lightly armoured and armed. Medium tanks were also relatively fast, but weighed anything up to 15 tons and were more heavily armoured and armed. Heavy tanks weighed anything up to forty tons and were very heavily armoured and heavily armed.

Then, after a number of exercises and consultations in 1934, the War Office published a new definition of the roles that British tanks should be able to fulfil in any coming war. This definition was significant, because it identified three different types of tank required to fill the main roles and this in turn influenced British tank design for almost a decade.

Light tanks would be retained and were intended to supplement cavalry in their traditional missions of scouting, reconnaissance and the exploitation of breakthroughs in the enemy front line (some British cavalry units retained their horses up to 1941). Infantry Tanks were intended to satisfy the needs of

Army tank units. Heavily armoured, they were primarily intended to provide direct support to advancing infantry. Infantry tanks did not require high speed but they were expected to be able to withstand attacks by enemy guns and to be armed with guns capable of destroying pillboxes and strongpoints. Cruiser Tanks were completely new and were primarily intended to for flanking and breakthrough, and to fulfil that role they also needed to be highly mobile on and off-road but also to be able to effectively fight enemy armour if necessary.

Once these new definitions had been agreed upon, one thing that immediately became obvious was that the British Army had no Infantry or Cruiser tanks. A few of the lozenge-shaped behemoths from World War One remained in service for a few years afterwards, but the only new design heavy tank design Britain had worked on since then was the A1E1 Independent, and that never got further than the prototype stage. The Medium Tanks then in service, principally the Medium Mark I and the slightly improved Medium Mark II, weren't fast (15 mph and 12 mph, respectively) and their main armament, the Ordnance QF 3 pounder, was based on a 1903 naval weapon and was not particularly effective as an anti-tank gun. If Britain were to have Cruiser tanks capable of fulfilling the new role, these would have to be entirely new designs. The only logical place to find new designs was Britain's only company active in tank design: Vickers - Armstrong.

The man in charge of technical developments at Vickers at that time was John Valentine Carden, one of the most prolific and respected British tank designers of the inter-war period. Carden had worked in the automotive industry before the war where he was a Captain in the British Army. He served in the Army Service Corps where he became familiar with tracked vehicles such as the Holt Tractors that were used for towing heavy guns. After the war, he formed his own sports-car company, but achieved little commercial success. In 1923, Carden met another man who had served as a Captain during the war, Vivian Graham Loyd. Both were talented engineers and they decided to form a new company dedicated to producing military vehicles.

Carden-Loyd was established in 1925 and soon began producing a range of two-man tankettes. These were well-designed and reliable and one model, the Mk.VI, sold more than four hundred and fifty examples to customers around the world. That may not sound particularly impressive, but at a time when most countries were cutting back on military expenditure, it represented a remarkable commercial success. In 1928, Carden-Loyd was bought by Vickers and by 1934, Carden was the Technical Director of Vickers. Carden was so highly regarded by the War Office that no interference was allowed in his design of the A9.

A Carden-Loyd Two-Man tankette.

Image: Imperial War Museum via Wikimedia Commons

Carden had worked on the design for the Medium Mk. III, but that tank had never gone into production.

With a growing recognition of the need to re-equip the British Army, at least it looked as though the new Cruiser tank design stood at least a reasonable chance of being produced in numbers.

The specification against which the new tank would be designed was produced by the War Office Directorate of Tank Design. This group received input from a number of sources including the Mechanisation Experimental Establishment and the Mechanisation Board (both established in 1934). The responsibility of these latter groups was to examine the tactical requirements of the British Army and translate these into operational requirements.

Despite its name, the Directorate of Tank Design generally did not design tanks. Instead it took the operational requirements defined by the Mechanisation Board and passed these on to the Department of Tank Design which produced from these a detailed technical specification that could then be issued through the General Staff Office and distributed to commercial companies. These would then lead to design proposals that would be reviewed by the Department of Tank Design and then passed on to the Mechanisation Board. Both these groups might suggest changes or improvements to the design and only once these had been incorporated and the design resubmitted might the Mechanisation Board authorise the construction of one or more prototypes which could then be given to the Mechanisation Experimental Establishment for evaluation and testing. This, almost inevitably, would result in additional request for changes.

Overall this was a slow, bureaucratic and cumbersome process that placed all the risk of undertaking a new design on commercial companies who might, or might not, then receive orders for prototypes and perhaps even production models of the new tank. It had not led to the successful development of a new medium or heavy tank since the introduction of the Medium Mk. II almost ten years before.

By the time that they started to consider the design for what would become the A9, Vickers had already been involved in two attempts to create a new British Medium Tank. Neither the A6 nor the A7 had gone beyond the prototype stage. Then main problems were that the weight of these tanks required the use of a complex linked pair of engines and both were provided with conventional suspension systems that proved unreliable in use. Trials of both from 1929 – 1932 showed that they were unsatisfactory overall, but both included features that the War Office liked. In particular, both had three-man main turrets, something that was quite unusual for the period. This meant that the commander was freed from the need to aim or load the main gun and this was felt to be a useful feature.

The Vickers A7E1 in 1931. It had problems, mainly in its fragile suspension, but the army liked the concept of a three-man turret.

Image: Imperial War Museum via Wikimedia Commons

Design

The A9

Although the concept of a Cruiser tank was something entirely new, at least in terms of the British Army, Carden was not given an entirely free hand to design what he liked. The design of the new tank would be constrained by a whole range of requirements and restrictions included in specification A9 issued by the General Staff Office (the British Army classed tracked vehicles as "A-type" and wheeled vehicles as "B-type) in 1935.

Some of these constraints were fixed. For example, all British tanks had to be capable of being transported by rail car, which meant that their overall width had to fit within the limits of the standard British railway gauge. All British tanks also had to be sufficiently light that they could be easily transported overseas on ships and so that they could safely use standard military bridges.

Other constraints had developed by custom and practice. For example, on all previous British tanks, the fighting compartment, containing the crew, engine, transmission and armament, was located wholly between the tracks. This gave a lower overall profile, but, in combination with the width limit for rail transport, meant a maximum size for the turret ring which in turn limited the size of the turret and of the main gun it could contain.

In terms of the new Cruiser tank, the most important single constraint was cost. There simply wasn't a great deal of money available for the design and construction of the new tank. It is claimed that in early and informal discussions about the new Cruiser, Carden was asked to provide a design for a *reasonably cheap tank.*" It was certainly true that the War Office used a simple formula for assessing the cost of any tank by weight: tanks should cost no more than £1,000 per ton. Wherever possible, the new design should use existing components to reduce cost.

The hull of the new tank would be constructed from riveted plates of steel. It was relatively small at just one hundred inches wide and two hundred and thirty inches long. Maximum armour thickness was just 14mm on the hull front and mantlet, sufficient to provide protection against light machine gun fire, but not against anything heavier. In other places the armour was even thinner: on the hull floor, for example, it was just 6mm thick. The thin armour was necessary to meet the overall weight requirement of just 12 tons that formed part of the War Office specification and was needed to enable the tank to reach a reasonable top speed.

Initially, Carden wanted to use a Rolls-Royce engine in this tank, but for reasons of cost and because the Rolls-Royce engine selected did not produce sufficient power, an existing petrol engine created by the Associated Equipment Company (AEC) which built trucks and coaches was later selected instead. The 9½ litre, six-cylinder A179 engine already used on buses produced 150bhp and drove the rear sprockets via a 5-speed Meadows No.22 manual gearbox.

Fitting the larger AEC engine into the cramped engine compartment did cause problems. The rear hull was redesigned to accept the AEC engine but the cooling fan and the radiator had to be placed on opposite sides of the compartment with the engine between them. The fan drew in outside air from louvers in the upper rear hull and then blew this air towards the radiator. The air passed over the hot engine and even hotter exhaust on the way to the radiator and as a result, was anything but cool. Engine overheating remained a problem throughout the service life of the A9 and the similarly designed A10.

Suspension was a modified version of a proprietary suspension design owned by Vickers. Sidney Horstmann had run his own company, Slow Motion Suspensions Ltd., which designed and built suspension systems used on several British tanks.

Horstman "Slow-Motion" suspension on a British Light Tank Mk. II.

Image: Imperial War Museum via Wikimedia Commons

This suspension system got its name, apparently, because tanks so fitted were less liable to the violent pitching that affected tanks with conventional suspension using stiff springs. Vickers bought Slow Motion Suspensions Ltd in the late 1920s and used Horstmann-type suspension on a number of its tank designs. On the A9, the suspension was based on Horstmann's ideas but with input from John Carden. This suspension is sometimes referred to as *"slow-motion"* or as Carden's *"bright-idea"* suspension.

On the A9, the suspension comprised two bogies on each side, with each bogie supporting one large and two smaller rubber-tyred road wheels. Each bogie utilised a single spring and a Newton hydraulic shock absorber to provide suspension movement and damping. This design had the advantage that the complete bogie assemblies could easily be removed for repair or replacement, but it had the disadvantage that it was not particularly robust. Cracked and broken suspension components and road wheels would feature throughout the service life of the A9.

The relatively narrow tracks lacked grousers: external extensions that extend the surface area of the track, reducing ground pressure and improving traction. They ran over the road wheels, a rear sprocket, a front idler (which was identical to the smaller of the two road wheels) and three rubber-covered return rollers.

The tracks proved problematic. They gave poor performance on rough terrain and were of complex design, derived from the tracks designed for the A7. To save weight, each main track-plate casting featured a large, rectangular opening. As a result, the tracks were prone to breakage after prolonged use off-road, especially on rocky ground. Because they were narrow, they also tended to twist in sharp turns and this often resulted in a thrown track. In service, track pins often broke or worked loose. In response, these pins were sometimes welded in place, but if this didn't work, the welded pins meant that it took even longer to repair or replace a track.

Another recurring problem that was never entirely solved was overheating of the brakes. The brake drums were move to the outside face of the rear idlers where they received more cooling air, but the overheating problem persisted, severely limited the ability of the A9 to manoeuvre quickly.

The turret for the new design was derived from the turret created for the abortive A7E3 and, like that tank, retained the three-man layout that the War Office had approved. On the A9, turret traverse was provided by a hydraulic system, the first time that this had been provided on a British tank. The design of this hydraulic system was borrowed from turrets designed for the Wellington bomber, which were also manufactured by Vickers.

A 2-Pdr. gun fitted to a Valentine Tank, also designed by Vickers. One of the padded supports for elevation can be seen just in front of the gunner's right shoulder.

Image: Imperial War Museum via Wikimedia Commons

As in virtually every British tank of World War Two, there was no mechanical means of elevating the main gun within the turret. The gun was treated like a giant rifle, with padded supports that rested on the gunner's shoulders. Elevation was set by the simple expedient of the gunner bending or straightening his legs.

In the British Army, it was believed that this approach allowed greater accuracy while firing on the move, but experience in combat suggested the opposite. It was virtually impossible to accurately sight the main gun while the tank was moving, especially over rough ground. As in most tanks of World War Two, accurate fire was only possible when the tank was stationery.

The gun itself was to be a modified version of the Ordnance QF 2-pdr. anti-tank gun. This weapon was also developed by Vickers in response to a War Office specification issued in 1934. While the A9 was being designed in 1935, the QF 2-pdr, represented the state-of-the-art in anti-tank weapon design. It was comparable to anti-tank guns being produced in Germany, though it was notably heavier than the German 37mm Pak 36. This gun fired a 2.4lb (40mm) projectile at over 2,500 fps and with an effective range of around 600yds. It was capable of penetrating up to

2 inches of armour at a range of 500yds. Its relatively small calibre meant that high explosive and smoke shells were not really effective, and almost no high explosive or smoke shells were ever made available for tanks equipped with this weapon.

The Ordnance QF 2-Pdr. Anti-Tank gun from which the main gun in the A9 was derived.

Image: Imperial War Museum via Wikimedia Commons

Though the 2-pdr. was provided for fighting enemy armour, it wasn't necessarily intended as the Cruiser tank's main weapon. The Cruiser was primarily envisaged as being used for exploitation and breakthrough, and doctrine suggested that fighting enemy tanks was only an incidental part of this role which would mainly involve dealing with enemy infantry. This view was widely accepted in the mid-1930s and the A9s contemporaries were designed with the same role in mind. For example, a German Army report in 1936 identified the role envisaged for the Panzer III, the German equivalent of the Cruisers:

> "The PzKpfw III is the assault tank (Sturmwagen), an "armored infantryman" (gepanzerte Infanterist) which wins the mobile battle with the annihilating power of its machine guns. The 3.7cm gun has been added to deal with the threat of an armoured opponent."

To make the A9 more effective in an anti-infantry role, it received its most notable feature: two additional turrets on the front hull, each housing a single machine gun. This followed the practice of earlier Vickers designs such as the A1 Independent.

The driver's position on the A9 was in the centre of the front hull, protected by an armoured box. On either side of this position were the two lightly-armoured, manually traversed circular turrets, each provided with a Vickers .303 water-cooled machine gun. A third Vickers machine gun was mounted co-axially in the main turret.

A trainee driver sits between the machine gun turrets in an A9 of the 53rd Training Regiment, Royal Armoured Corps, at Tidworth in October 1940.

Image: Imperial War Museum via Wikimedia Commons

The provision of these extra machine gun turrets certainly gave the A9 formidable anti-infantry capability, but it also presented a few significant problems. The siting of turrets either side of the driver's armoured box on the front hull created potentially lethal shot traps for armour-piercing rounds. Each of the two turrets was permanently manned, giving this fairly small tank a crew of six. This meant that the interior was very cramped indeed and there was no division in the fighting compartment. The provision of the extra turrets accorded with current military doctrine in the mid-1930s, but when the A9 was used in combat, they were found to be of little practical use.

In order to reduce costs, there was little that was truly new in Carden's design for the A9. The engine, transmission, suspension, turret, main gun and machine guns were all existing components or derived from existing designs. Only the boat-shaped hull with its two auxiliary turrets was a wholly new design. The design proposal was approved by the War Office in late 1935. However, in December 1935, John Carden (who by this time was Sir John Carden, 6th Baronet of Templemore, Tipperary) was killed in an air crash and subsequent work on the A9 was carried out under the direction of another senior engineer in Vickers, Leslie Little.

The Prototype A9E1. Note the conical covers over the machine gun turrets, bulky commander's cupola and 3-Pdr. main gun.

Image: Imperial War Museum via Wikimedia Commons

The first prototype was delivered to the British Army for evaluation in April 1936 as the A9E1. This was provided with the Rolls-Royce engine originally envisaged by Carden and a QF 3-pdr. gun as the 2-pdr. was still in final development. It also differed from the final version in having conical covers over the machine-gun turrets, the exhaust mounted on the left track-guard rather than on the rear hull and a sloped rear plate on the turret. The prototype weighted twelve and a half tons, just over the 12-ton limit specified by the War Office.

Testing showed that the 120bhp engine in the prototype simply was not powerful enough to provide the required top speed of 25mph. Leslie Little wanted to replace it with an AEC diesel engine. Diesel engines are intrinsically safer in military vehicles because their fuel is less flammable. The British Army had little experience with diesel fuel and there were concerns about the need for separate fuel supplies for diesel-engine vehicles. For these reasons, Little was over-ruled by the War Office and in subsequent versions of the A9, the 150bhp A179 petrol engine was fitted. This gave the required top speed of 25mph on roads and around 15mph off-road with a maximum range of around 150 miles.

Testing also revealed that the bulky turret cupola was not satisfactory and it was replaced with a two-piece hatch incorporating a Vickers Gundlach periscope in one of the hatches. Additional observation slits were added to the machine gun turrets to improve visibility, the front hull was redesigned and the exhaust was moved to the rear hull. The rear hull was redesigned to accept the larger A179 engine. The prototype was also used for deep-wading trials, apparently successfully crossing the River Stour at Christchurch. Unfortunately, the riveted hull leaked badly during the trials and no production version of the A9 seems to have been provided with deep wading gear.

Another view of the A9E1 prototype.

Image: Imperial War Museum via Wikimedia Commons

With these changes, the War Office was satisfied, though the performance of the prototype left much to be desired. The narrow tracks proved ineffective on rough ground and, even worse, if the tank was manoeuvred violently, it was prone to throwing or breaking tracks. The problems with engine and brake overheating were noted, but the design was not changed. The political situation in Europe was worsening and the prospect of a war with Germany was becoming more definite.

Although design of the improved A13 Cruiser was nearing completion, the only tank actually ready for production was the A9. On the basis that it was better to have at least some less than perfect cruisers in service rather than wait for the next design to reach maturity, the first order for 50 A9s was placed by the War Office in early 1938.

This tank was given the War Office title "*Tank, Cruiser Mk. I*", though it also retained the A9 designation. The notion of naming tanks was not in vogue in the British Army in 1938. In late 1940, when it was decided that names were helpful for the rapid identification of tanks in radio messages, the name "*Krait*" was suggested for the A9 (the krait is a highly venomous snake found in South and Southeast Asia). By the time that this was finally agreed in 1941, the A9 was virtually obsolete and this tank was never formally given a name within the British Army.

The A10

The design of the A10 was virtually concurrent with that of the A9, beginning with a War Office specification in 1934 and initially being worked on by John Carden before being taken over by Leslie Little. The initial concept was rather vague. Perhaps this was to be a new Medium Tank, or a Heavy Cruiser or perhaps even a Light Infantry Tank? Just as with the A9 there was some urgency involved to get the new tank into service, so it was agreed to use the existing lower hull and mechanicals from the A9.

The specification for the A10 was similar to that provided for the A9 with one significant difference: it called for frontal armour at least one inch thick and accepted that this would mean a lower overall top speed. This thickness of armour would not provide complete protection against German anti-tank weapons, but it would at least resist fire from the 20mm cannon fitted to the Panzer II. During development of the A10 prototype, the specification was revised to require two inches of frontal armour. However, it was clear that the A9 design, and especially the engine, suspension and transmission simply could not cope with the additional weight, so it was agreed that work would continue on developing a tank with just one inch of armour.

The A10E1 prototype. The front hull was completely redesigned before production began.

Image: Imperial War Museum via Wikimedia Commons

The first A10 prototype, the A10E1 was delivered by Vickers in July 1937, more than one year after delivery of the A9 prototype. The A10 had the same turret (though with thicker frontal armour), gun, co-axial Vickers machine gun, engine, transmission, tracks and suspension as the A9, with the only changes being made to the front hull by removing the two machine gun turrets. The additional armour increased overall weight by over one ton, reducing top speed on road to 16mph and to less than 10mph off-road.

The engine in the A10 was the same A179 fitted to the A9, though, just as on the A9, the prototype was fitted with a Rolls-Royce engine that proved even less capable of propelling the heavier A10 at a reasonable speed. The main gun remained the QF 2-Pdr. supplemented by one co-axial Vickers water-cooled machine gun.

A second prototype was delivered later in 1937, A10E2, though this was nothing to do with the Cruiser tank program. Vickers was already working on a private-venture design for a much heavier infantry tank. The second prototype was intended to see whether the engine, transmission and suspension designed for the A9/A10 could be used for a heavier tank. That second prototype eventually evolved into the hugely successful A12 Valentine Infantry Tank, which would account for almost one quarter of all tanks produced by Britain during World War Two. With A12 development in hand, it was agreed that the A10 would become a Heavy Cruiser Tank and not an Infantry Tank.

After testing, a number of changes were made to the A10 before production began. The bulky commander's cupola was replaced with a two-piece hatch incorporating a periscope, the front hull was revised with the driver's position moved to the left and a hull machine gunner's position added on the right. Instead of the bulky Vickers water-cooled machine gun, the hull position was provided with a lighter, air-cooled BESA machine gun produced by the Birmingham Small Arms Company (BSA). This belt-fed gun, a licensed copy of the Czech ZB-53, was lighter and more accurate than the Vickers machine gun. But production of the BESA machine gun did not begin until 1939, and many early A10s left the factory without a bow machine gun.

One other change to the production version was the addition of an extra 35-gallon fuel tank between the driver and bow machine gunner, something that must have caused more than a little concern in combat. Even with the addition of this extra tank, the operational range of the heavier A10 was only around 100 miles.

With the changes in place, the production A10 weighed just over 14 tons, 1.5 tons heavier than the

A9, but with the same engine, transmission and suspension. Overall, the A10 was disappointing. It was notably slower than the A9 and its additional armour still didn't give adequate protection against German anti-tank or tank weapons. As a compromise, it was not a success. It was not sufficiently heavily armoured to act as an Infantry Tank nor was the QF 2-Pdr. gun well suited to that role. But its extra armour made it too slow to be effective as a Cruiser. It was accepted into service simply because the design was complete and it could be produced quickly, whatever its failings.

It also had the same reliability issues with the engine, suspension and tracks as the A9, all made even worse by the additional weight. After going through several potential different titles including "*Tank, Cruiser, Heavy Mk I*" and "*Tank, Cruiser A10 Mk I*", this tank was eventually given the War Office title "*Tank, Cruiser Mk. II*", though it also retained the A10 designation. Like the A9, it was never given a formal name in British Service.

Variants

A10 Cruiser Tank Mk. IIA

The need to provide two different types of machine gun ammunition (for the co-axial Vickers and bow BESA) was an issue for early A10s. To overcome this problem, in the spring of 1940, a new version of the A10 was introduced, designated the *Tank, Cruiser Mk. IIA*. This was identical to the previous version other than for the addition of an armoured radio housing and the installation of Gun Mount No. 3 in the turret, which allowed fitment of the QF 2-Pdr. with a co-axial BESA machine gun identical to the bow machine gun. Most A10s manufactured were Mk. IIA versions.

Close Support (CS) Version

While the QF 2-Pdr. was, at the time it was introduced, an effective anti-tank weapon, the fact that it could not fire an effective high-explosive (HE) or smoke shell was a notable drawback. The use of smoke shells in particular was seen as an essential part of tank operations in the British Army and, in order to overcome this deficiency, a number of A9s and A10s were produced in Close Support (CS) configuration.

The CS versions were identical the standard version other than for the installation of a 3.7 in (94 mm) howitzer in the turret, replacing the QF 2-Pdr gun. This was a derivation of a World War One field gun and, despite its title, it was not a howitzer, being in effect a breech-loaded mortar. The main function of this gun was to fire smoke shells and the typical CS ammunition loadout comprised 40 smoke shells and only a few HE shells. A proportion of both the A9 and A10 were produced in CS configuration.

A9s and A10s in North Africa

Tanks sent to North Africa were modified by improving cooling and filtration systems, but these changes were not visible externally. Some (but not all) of these A9s and A10s were fitted with side-skirts on the left side to protect the suspension and running gear from the abrasive effects of sand.

Experimental Bridgelayer

One A10 was experimentally converted by having the turret removed and replaced with a hydraulically extended Scissors Bridge 30ft, Number 1 on a structure attached to the hull. Trials suggested that the additional weight of this equipment put even more strain on the already stressed suspension, transmission and engine, and no more than one A10 seems to have been converted in this way.

Production and Operational Deployment

A9 Production

Although testing and evaluation of the prototype A9E1 had shown that the new Cruiser was far from perfect, the British Army needed new tanks as quickly as possible. An initial order for 50 A9s was placed in early 1938 and was undertaken at the Elswick Works near Newcastle-under-Lyme, owned by Vickers. Due to production delays, the first completed tank was not handed over to the army until almost one year later, in January 1939. The last A9 was delivered from Elswick in February 1940. The 50 tanks produced by the Elswick works were assigned War Department numbers from T3493 - T3542. It was clear that another additional manufacturer was needed to produce the new tank in sufficient numbers.

Harland and Wolff, based in Belfast in Northern Ireland, was one of the UK's largest shipbuilders in the first half of the 20th century. They created warships for the Royal Navy and commercial ships including the ill-fated Titanic. During the 1920s, a downturn in shipbuilding led the company to expand into new areas. They began the manufacture of railway locomotives and, through an agreement with Short Brothers in 1936, created Short & Harland Limited to produce aircraft including the Handley Page Hereford bomber and the Short Sunderland flying boat.

By 1938, the company was looking to expand into tank manufacture and design. One of the first orders that the new division attracted was for the manufacture of 75 A9 tanks. By this time the need for a CS version of the tank had become clear, so 35 of the tanks ordered from Harland & Wolff were in this configuration. The first A9 was delivered by June 1939 and the final A9 was delivered in July 1940. The 75 tanks produced by Harland & Wolff were assigned War Department numbers from T7196 - T7270.

These 125 tanks delivered by Elswick and Harland & Wolff represented total production of the A9.

A10 Production

Because the Elswick works owned by Vickers was already committed to A9 production, an initial order for just 10 A10s was placed directly with Vickers. These tanks began to be delivered in late 1939 and were assigned War Department numbers from T8091 - T8100. Because of the urgent need for these tanks to be provided quickly, and because neither Vickers nor Harland and Wolff were able to produce more, production orders were placed with several companies with no previous experience of manufacturing tanks. Inevitably, this led to delays in production.

A much larger order for 75 tanks was placed with a Vickers subsidiary, the Metropolitan Cammell Carriage and Wagon Company, a manufacturer of railway carriages and wagons based in Birmingham. These tanks were assigned War Department numbers from T9191 - T9265. Another order for 75 tanks was placed with the Birmingham Railway Carriage and Wagon Company, another Birmingham-based manufacturer of railway rolling stock. These tanks were assigned War Department numbers from T5909 - T5983. Finally, the largest order of all, for 100 tanks, was placed with R. W. Crabtree and Sons, a manufacturer of printing machines based in Huddersfield in the North of England. Before production in Huddersfield got properly underway, this order was reduced to just 10 tanks, assigned War Department numbers from T15115 - 15124.

A total of 170 A10s were produced in total. Only the first 45 tanks were in Mk II configuration and all subsequent production was of the Mk IIA. Only 30 of the CS variant were built, all at the Metropolitan Cammell Carriage and Wagon Company.

The final delivery of A10s, from R. W. Crabtree and Sons, took place in the summer of 1941, by which time this tank was already being phased-out of operational use.

Operational Deployment
France

By the time that war was declared on September 1st 1939, the British Army was critically short of tanks and almost completely unready for war. In March of that year Lord Gort, the man who would command the British Expeditionary Force (BEF) in France, told the Secretary of State for War, Leslie Hore-Belisha, that: *"It would be murder to send our Field Force abroad to fight against a first-class Power."* Despite this, and within two weeks of the declaration of war, the BEF was sent to France in the expectation of a German attack.

Fewer than 150 Cruiser and Infantry tanks were in service at that time. The first A9s had been delivered to British units in January of that year but overall numbers were still small. Some of the Infantry Tanks were sent to France with the BEF but the Cruisers were instead provided to units of the 1st Armoured Division, at that time still based in the UK.

The Mobile Division was first formed in 1937 and in 1938 was renamed as the 1st Armoured Division. On paper, this was a formidable force, including two light and one heavy brigade. However, while the division was equipped with light and cruiser tanks, it lacked mechanised infantry support. This was the result of British tactical doctrine, which saw such armoured units as a direct replacement for cavalry, intended for to operate, independently, *en-masse* and without infantry support to fight enemy armoured formations, exploit breakthroughs and to pursue broken and retreating enemy forces. There was no real appreciation of the need for the sort of combined-arms units such as the Panzer Divisions fielded by Germany. The 1st Armoured Division was still training and still receiving its new Cruisers when the war began. The assumption was that the combination of the French army and the BEF to oppose any German attack would allow time for training to be completed before it would be necessary to send the Cruisers into battle.

In the British Army in 1939, cavalry units retained their names, but were referred to as regiments, although they were battalion-size units. Most Cruiser tanks were given to cavalry regiments. Battalions of the Royal Tank Regiment (re-named from the Royal Tank Corps in early 1939) were numbered sequentially. While some RTR Battalions were provided with Cruisers, others were established as infantry tank units and equipped with light tanks and the A11 Infantry Tank Mk. I (Matilda) and A12 Infantry Tank Mk. II (Matilda II).

In May 1940, following the German invasion, it was decided that two of the three brigades of the 1st Armoured Division were to be sent to France immediately even though they were not fully trained nor provided with a full complement of tanks. The situation had become so serious, so quickly that something had to be done to stop the Germans. The brigades sent to France were the 2nd (Light) brigade under the command of Brigadier R. L. McCreery comprising the 2nd Queen's Bays, 9th Queen's Royal Lancers and 10th Royal Hussars and the 3rd (Heavy) Brigade under the command of Brigadier J.G. Crocker comprising the 2nd, 3rd and 5th Battalions of The Royal Tank Regiment. Most of these units were understrength and all comprised Light and Cruiser tanks. By that time, deliveries of the new A13 Cruiser Tank in both Mk. III and improved MK IV form had begun and most units included a mix of A9, A10 and both versions of the A13.

The Cruisers of the 1st Armoured Division were the first of this new type of tank to be sent to France, but they were not the first British tanks to face German forces there. The 4th Battalion RTR had arrived in France in September 1939 with the BEF. It was joined in early May 1940 by 7th Battalion RTR. These battalions were involved in combat with German forces following the German invasion of Holland and Belgium on 10th May but both were infantry tank battalions and neither was equipped with Cruisers.

By the time that 1st Armoured Division arrived in France, the situation facing the British Expeditionary Force (BEF) was already grave. German forces were pushing through Holland and Belgium and into France: Dutch forces had surrendered on 18th May and the Belgians would follow on 28th May. In addition to the push through Belgium, German Panzer Divisions had also crossed the Meuse after attacking through the Ardennes and were sweeping north-west at bewildering speed. The 3rd Royal Tank Regiment was embarked to Calais, while the rest of the 1st Armoured Division landed at Cherbourg on 22nd May 1940. By that time, German Panzer Divisions had arrived at the Channel Coast, cutting off the BEF and a large part of the French Army in North-eastern France.

The Brigades of the 1st Armoured Division sent to France were hurled into combat before they were fully prepared in a desperate attempt to stop the rampaging German Panzer Divisions. In many cases, crews had little time to become familiar with their new tanks and there were shortages of spares and equipment: some A10s arrived in France without their BESA machine guns. When 3rd Battalion RTR arrived in Calais, they discovered that all the HE shells for their A9 CS had been left behind in England. Almost none of the A9s and A10s sent to France would return.

North Africa

At the same time that the Mobile Division which would become the 1st Armoured Division was being formed in Britain, another British armoured force was established in Egypt. Mobile Division (Egypt) was initially placed under the command of tank theorist Major-General Sir Percy Hobart and comprised four armoured regiments: 7th Queen's Own Hussars, 8th King's Royal Irish Hussars, 11th Hussars and 1st Battalion RTR. When the war began, 6th and 2nd Battalions RTR also joined the 7th Armoured Division. In early 1940, this unit was re-named 7th Armoured Division and, under this name it would fight throughout the campaign in North Africa and gain fame as the *Desert Rats*.

When World War Two began in September 1939, Mobile Force (Egypt) had just 65 tanks instead of its full complement of 220. All were light tanks and many were obsolete types such as the Vickers Mk. II, first introduced in 1931. By early 1940, these had been supplemented by the arrival of first A9 Cruisers and then by A10s.

On 11th June 1940, Italy declared war on Britain and soon, 7th Armoured Division was involved in combat with Italian forces. In combat with Italian forces, the British Cruiser tanks proved more than adequate and gained a number of impressive victories. These continued until March 1941 and the arrival of German forces of the Africa Korps under the command of Field Marshal Erwin Rommel. Faced with improved German tanks, the A9s and A10s proved vulnerable. By the time that German forces entered combat in North Africa, 7th Armoured Division had over 70 A9s and 50 A10s in service. By late 1941, the A9 was withdrawn from active service and re-classified as a training tank, though a few continued to be used in North Africa in fixed defensive positions such as those around the port city of Tobruk. The A10 lasted a little longer, with some A10s still being used on the island of Cyprus as late as early 1943.

Greece

In October 1940, Italian forces launched an invasion of Albania and Greece. This invasion was repulsed by Greek forces but, in April 1941, German forces launched successful invasions of Yugoslavia and Greece. Anticipating this German attack, a British Expeditionary Force was sent to Greece in March 1941. This force included 3rd Battalion RTR equipped with A10 tanks.

This brief Balkan campaign resulted in another disastrous defeat for the British with the bulk of British and Commonwealth forces being evacuated ahead of the German advance at the end of April 1941. None of the A10 tanks sent to Greece with 3rd Battalion RTR were recovered.

Enemies and Allies

Before looking at how the A9 and A10 fared in combat, we will examine similar tanks and other weapons on the battlefields on which they were used, both those of Britain's enemies and its Allies. During the period during which these tanks were used operationally, the United States was neutral and took no part in combat and the Soviet Union was in alliance with Germany, so these British tanks never shared the battlefield with any American or Russian tanks. For that reason, comparisons will be made only with weapons used by Germany, Italy and France.

Germany

German rearmament and the expansionist intentions of the Nazi regime were the main drivers for the creation of the A9 and the A10. The Cruiser tanks were designed specifically to take part in a war in Europe against Nazi Germany and her allies, so German tank development was closely studied in Britain.

The closest German equivalent to the A9 and A10 was the Panzer III. Design of this tank originated in a specification issued by the German General Staff in

1934 for a tank capable of engaging enemy armour, with a weight of no more than 10 tons and a top speed of 40kmh (25mph). The first version of this tank, the Ausführung (meaning "*model*", usually abbreviated to Ausf.) A, was introduced in August 1937 and was similar in specification to the A9, with coil spring suspension and armour that ranged from 14.5mm thickness on the hull front to just 5mm on the underside. Armament was a derivation of the German Pak 36 anti-tank gun in a three-man turret and was similar in range and penetrating ability to the QF 2-Pdr. fitted to the A9 and A10.

Just 10 Panzer III Ausf. A were produced and the lack of armoured protection and fragile suspension were quickly recognised as inadequate in the Wehrmacht. The first mass-produced version of this tank, the Ausf. E, was provided with greatly improved and more reliable torsion-bar suspension and hull and turret armour up to 30mm thick. This version, which was used by German units during fighting in France in 1940, also had a more powerful engine which gave an improved top speed of 45kmh despite the weight of additional armour.

It is interesting to contrast the rapid development and improvement of the Panzer III with the creation of the A9 and A10. The initial Ausf. A model of the Panzer III was little better than the A9 and in particular its complex suspension was fragile.

The Panzer III Ausf. D (seen here during the invasion of Poland) still had complex leaf-spring suspension, but this was refined before volume production of the Ausf. E.

Image: Deutsches Bundesarchiv Bild 101I-318-0083-32 via Wikimedia Commons

In just two years, improvement and development produced the Ausf. E with robust and reliable torsion-bar suspension which was in service by the time that war began. This model was superior to both the A9 and A10 and, more importantly, reliable and highly mobile. There was no attempt to improve or upgrade the A9 or A10 after they entered service. Instead, completely new designs of Cruiser tank were quickly rushed into production, each bringing its own crop of new problems.

When the British Cruiser tanks met the German Afrika Korps in 1941, they were up against the Panzer III Ausf. G and H with even more armour and, in a few cases, armed with the more powerful 5 cm KwK 38 L/42 main gun. At that point the British tanks were hopelessly outclassed.

Of course, although the Panzer III was in many ways the direct equivalent of the British Cruisers, it wasn't the only German tank they faced. The Panzer IV was originally designed as a support tank. It was armed with a short-barrelled 7.5cm main gun designed to tackle enemy strongpoints but, unlike the British Infantry Tanks, it was still highly mobile with a top speed of around 25mph. Like the Panzer III, it underwent continual upgrades and the Ausf. D and E versions that the BEF faced in France were provided with up to 30mm of armour and were extremely reliable.

A Panzer I Ausf. B of SS-Leibstandarte "Adolf Hitler" in Paris, 1940.

Image: Deutsches Bundesarchiv Bild 101I-256-1234-06

Germany also fielded the Panzer I and II in France and the Panzer II in North Africa. The Panzer I was a light, two-man tank armed only with machine guns while the Panzer II had a crew of three and was armed with the 2 cm KwK 30 L/55 auto-cannon. This relatively small-calibre weapon was nevertheless capable of penetrating the frontal armour on the A9, though not the A10. The Ausf. C version faced by the

BEF in France was provided with 14mm of frontal and side armour, similar to the A9. It is notable that all versions of the Panzer II were mechanically reliable and faster than either British Cruisers with the Ausf. E model capable of 35mph.

The German tanks that the A9 and A10 faced in France were not overwhelmingly better armed or armoured. The advantage they had was that all had better off-road performance and all were significantly more reliable that their British counterparts. German tank crews were also well-trained and many of those that the BEF faced in France had previous combat experience from fighting in Poland. Probably the most significant advantage that German tanks enjoyed involved the tactics of their use. German tanks were not deployed in separate, all-tank formations as British doctrine suggested. German Panzer Divisions instead included mechanized infantry and, critically, organic anti-tank capability.

A Pak 36 Anti-Tank gun.

Image: Deutsches Bundesarchiv Bild 101I-299-1831-26

The main German anti-tank gun in service in 1940/1941 was the Panzerabwehrkanone (Pak) 36. This 37mm weapon had performance equivalent to that of the British 2-Pdr. Over 9,000 Pak 36 guns were in service with the German Army when World War Two began. This gun was light and easily portable, something that worked well with German tactics of moving anti-tank guns up in support of advancing tanks. The Pak 36 was capable of penetrating the frontal armour on both the A9 and A10, though it proved ineffective against more heavily armoured British tanks such as the Matilda II.

Italy

Tank development in Italy lagged behind that of other European nations. It wasn't until 1938 that consideration was given for the first time to arming tanks with main guns capable of engaging enemy armour. Up to this point, all Italian tanks and tankettes were small, lightly armoured and armed only with machine guns. Development of new tanks was rushed and the Italian tanks that British forces faced in North Africa were notably inferior to their German counterparts. In addition to a number of light tanks and tankettes, the British faced three types of Italian Medium Tank in North Africa:

The Carro Armato M11/39 followed normal Italian tank naming convention. "Carro Armato" simply means "armoured vehicle", "M" stands for Medium, "11" is the tank's weight in tons and "39" is the year it entered service. The M11/39 was, like the A9, a tank of unusual design. The small revolving turret housed just two machine guns while the main armament, a Vickers-Terni 37 mm /L40 gun, was located in a fixed position on the front hull with just 15° of traverse available.

Closest to the camera are two Italian Carro Armato M11/39 tanks captured by Australian troops in Tobruk, January 1940. The furthest tank is the later M13/40.

Image: Australian War Memorial collections database via Wikimedia Commons

This made it very difficult for the main gun to be used to engage armoured targets, but this wasn't the M11/39s only flaw. Its riveted frontal armour was just 30mm thick and could be penetrated by the British QF 2-Pdr. even at that weapon's maximum range. The M11/39 was also relatively slow, with a top speed of less than 20mph on road and significantly less off-road. Its Vickers-derived suspension was fragile and the narrow tracks limited off-road use. This tank was also unreliable and none of the 100 M11/39s produced was fitted with a radio.

A Carro Armato M13/40 in North Africa.

Image: Deutsches Bundesarchiv Bild 101I-784-0209-15

The Carro Armato M13/40 was designed as a replacement for the M11/39, and it was significantly improved, though it too suffered from major faults. Its main armament, a derivation of the effective Cannone da 47/32 M35 anti-tank gun, was mounted conventionally in a rotating turret though this was hampered by having space for only two crew, meaning that the commander also had to aim and fire the main gun. A co-axial machine gun was supplemented by two more in a ball-mount on the front hull. Its frontal armour was around 30mm thick and the main gun on the M13/40 was capable of penetrating the frontal armour on both the A9 and A10 and it had a longer effective range than the QF 2-Pdr. However, it used the same engine and transmission as the M11/39 and so it was even slower than that tank and it suffered from many of the same reliability issues.

The Carro Armato M14/41 was also used in the North African campaign and appeared in 1941, in time to face the last British A9 and A10s before they were withdrawn from front-line service. It was essentially an upgrade to the M13/40, though the changes were limited to improved armour and the provision of a diesel engine to replace the petrol engine used in the earlier tank. The diesel engine gave this version slightly improved top speed, though it was still slower than the A9. Like the earlier tank, it was armed with the effective 47mm M35 main gun though this was still mounted in a small, two-man turret.

Italian forces in North Africa also fielded highly effective self-propelled guns including the Semovente da 75/18, based on the chassis of the M13/40, and Semovente da 47/32, based on the chassis of the L 6/40 light tank, but these did not enter service until early 1942, after the British A9s and A10s had been withdrawn from front-line service.

The principal Italian anti-tank gun in service in 1940/1941 was the Cannone da 47/32 mod. 1935. This was an effective weapon in the anti-tank role (it was also used as an infantry support gun) with performance equivalent to the British QF 2-Pdr. It was capable of penetrating the frontal armour on both the A9 and A10. Compared to other anti-weapons of the period, this weapon's main drawback was the lack of a gun shield to protect the crew from splinters and small-arms fire.

Looking at the specifications of these Italian tanks and guns, it is tempting to conclude that they should have been effective against the A9 and A10. But combat isn't simply a real-life game of Top Trumps where the weapon with the highest numbers always prevails. The main problem for Italian armoured forces wasn't the quality of their tanks and guns but the poor performance of their crews. This was generally a result of inadequate training. Some Italian tank crews for example, were sent into battle after receiving less than 25 days of training. Many were unfamiliar with even basic operation of equipment and this, combined with a shortage of radios, made them relatively ineffective in combat.

France

French tank development prior to World War Two was hampered by a lack of an effective tactical doctrine for the use of armoured vehicles. Initially, development focused on heavy, slow tanks designed as infantry support weapons and small, light tanks designed to fulfil the cavalry role. In the mid-1930s there was recognition of a need for independent armoured units. This led to the formation of the *Division Légère Mécanique* (Light Mechanized Divisions) and this in turn led to the identification of the need for a new type of tank, mobile and capable of fighting effectively against enemy armour. This was similar to the view in Britain that led to development of Cruiser tanks, but it led to the development of arguably the best tank in service in any Nation at the beginning of World War Two, the SOMUA S35.

In 1934 a specification was issued for a new tank suitable for use by the DLM. A subsidiary of Schneider, Société d'Outillage Mécanique et d'Usinage d'Artillerie (SOMUA) produced a proposal that was accepted and, in April 1935, the first prototype was accepted for testing. The first production tanks, with the designation SOMUA S35, began to be delivered to front-line units in 1938.

The design of the S35 was conventional, with a revolving turret containing the main gun attached to a hull superstructure that housed the crew, engine and transmission. Moreover, the hull was cast, an advanced technique used by very few early war tanks, providing frontal armour up to 47mm thick. The turret, also cast, was a derivation of the APX1 turret also used on the Char B1 heavy tank. The turret armour was up to 40mm thick. Dense armour meant that the tank weighed around 19 tons, considerably heavier than the 12.5-ton A9 and 14-ton A10. Despite this, the provision of a powerful, 190bhp SOMUA V-8 petrol engine gave it a top speed slightly better than the A9 and with a range of around 150 miles. The engine and transmission of the S35 proved to be reliable and its cast armour meant that, from the front, it could not be penetrated by the German Pak 36 anti-tank gun or by the 37mm main gun in the Panzer III.

The main gun fitted to the S35 was the 47 mm SA35 L/32. In addition to armour-piercing rounds, this gun also fired a useful 1.4 kg HE round. With a muzzle velocity of over 2,000 fps, this was the most effective and powerful main gun fitted to any early-war tank and it was capable of penetrating the frontal armour of all German tanks in 1940.

SOMUA S35 tanks captured near Dunkirk, May 1940.

Image: Deutsches Bundesarchiv Bild 121-0412

The main limitation of the S35 was its cramped turret. When fitted to the Char B1, the APX1 was a one-man turret that required the commander to load, aim and fire the main gun while retaining situational awareness and commanding other members of the crew. The provision of a slightly larger turret ring on the S35 meant that this became what was known as a

"*1½ man*" turret. There was just enough space for the radio operator, who normally sat next to the driver in the front of the hull, to squeeze his head and shoulders into the turret and to act as loader for the main gun. This did ease the workload for the commander slightly, but the need to aim and fire the main gun while commanding the tank made the S35 significantly less effective in combat than the British Cruisers and German Panzer III and IV with their three-man turrets.

The S35 also had issues with its suspension, which proved fragile when used off-road and vulnerable to enemy fire. Armoured skirts were provided to protect the suspension, but these meant that the suspension itself was difficult to repair in the field and that broken tracks were almost impossible to repair without access to a field workshop. Finally, though all S35s were designed to be provided with radios, only around 25% of the S35s used in the Battle of France in 1940 had these fitted, making combat command and control of tank units very difficult.

The three critical elements of tank capability are protection, firepower and mobility. The S35 probably had the best balance of all three on the outbreak of

World War Two. Its effectiveness was limited by the high workload placed on the commander, the lack of radios in many S35s and the way in which they were used, in small numbers rather than *en-masse*, meant that the almost 300 S35s in service at the time of the German invasion were unable to stop or even significantly slow the advancing Panzer Divisions.

In Combat

This chapter gives information about the use of A9 and A10 tanks in front-line service. It is by no means a comprehensive examination of every action in which these tanks took part, but rather an overview highlighting the abilities and limitations of these tanks when used in combat. In the *Further Reading* section, you will find information about other publications that provide more information about specific campaigns or battles.

France

When the decision was taken to send the 1st Armoured Division to France to support troops and tanks of the BEF already there, only two of the Division's three Brigades were fully equipped with tanks and support vehicles. These were the 2nd Light Brigade, under the command of Brigadier R. L. McCreery and the 3rd Heavy Brigade under the command of Brigadier J.G. Crocker. Each battalion comprised an HQ Squadron of Cruiser and CS Cruiser tanks and three squadrons of Cruiser or light tanks. In addition to A9s and A10s, the Cruisers used by these battalions also included the new A13 Cruiser Mk III and the A13 Mk II Cruiser Mk

IV. Many battalions featured a mixture of these Cruiser types.

The personnel of 1st Armoured Division were all too aware of the limitations of both the A9 and A10. Captain Dick Shattock, the Technical Adjutant of 3rd RTR wrote in a contemporary personal journal:

> "The battalion was equipped with A10 tanks, surely ranked as the worst in history. As an engineer I quickly realised this. The tracks broke every few miles, literally. The engines, ex-AEC London bus engines, were installed with the radiator cooling fan placed on one side of the tank, the radiator itself placed on the opposite side. The so-called cool air then passed over the overheated engine via the red-hot exhaust through the radiator."

He added:

> "The designers of the A10 must be in the pay of the Nazis."

Another Officer of 3rd RTR, Second Lieutenant Robert Crisp, was just as scathing about the unit's A10s:

> "They were ponderous square things like mobile pre-fab houses and just about as

flimsy. Their worst failing was their complete inability to move more than a mile or two in any sort of heavy going without breaking a track or shedding one on a sharp turn.[1]"

Despite the obvious shortcomings of their tanks, 3rd RTR was separated from the rest of 1st Armoured Division and sent to the port of Calais to support the British 30th Infantry Brigade in defending the city against the advancing German 1st Panzer Division.

The Battalion was equipped with 27 Cruiser tanks (a mixture of A9s, A10s and both marks of A13s) supported by 21 light tanks. The decision to send this unit to Calais was taken at short notice, and when it arrived on 21st May 1940, it was discovered that some ammunition, notably HE shells for the CS tanks, had been left behind. A few tanks had arrived direct from the factory before the unit embarked, and several cases A10s did not have their hull machine guns fitted: in some cases, plates were hastily welded over the openings in the front hull.

---

[1] Robert Crisp, *The Gods Were Neutral*, W.W. Norton, 1961

A9 tanks of 5ᵗʰ RTR, 1ˢᵗ Armoured Division on a training exercise in Surrey in 1940.

Image: Imperial War Museum via Wikimedia Commons

In the afternoon of 23ʳᵈ May, while advancing towards the village of Guines, several kilometres from Calais, the tanks of 3ʳᵈ RTR met Panzer II, II and IV of the 1ˢᵗ Panzer Division for the first time. The outcome was not a good baptism of fire for the new Cruisers.

> *"My own tank was a cruiser type A9, which only had a smoke howitzer and one MG on it. This was not encouraging, as I could only watch other tanks fighting and not hit back myself. Soon one tank after another was put*

out of action. It was obvious we were outgunned and outnumbered, and the only thing was to withdraw back to Calais. My tank would at least put down smoke so with its help, and the help of two other 'smoke tanks', we put down a smoke screen and withdrew to a ridge between Coquelles and Calais."

Major Reeves, 'B' Squadron, 3rd Royal Tank Regiment.

The tanks of 3rd RTR withdrew to the city and prepared to defend it against attacks from two Panzer Divisions: the 10th Panzer Division had also been instructed to join the attack on the city. For the remainder of what became known as the Siege of Calais, 3rd RTR tanks were used only in static, defensive positions. Enduring artillery strikes and air attack, the defenders of Calais were able to hold out for less than three days after initial contact with German units and the city fell on 26th May.

By that time, many of the personnel of 3rd RTR had either been evacuated directly from Calais or were making their way towards the main remaining BEF stronghold in northern France at Dunkirk. All the battalion's tanks were abandoned at Calais.

During the evacuation, one French unit took charge of some of the Cruiser tanks abandoned by 3rd RTR. The French 342nd Compagnie Autonome de Chars (Independent Tank Company) had taken part in the campaign in Norway, but had been forced to abandon its Hotchkiss H-39 and Renault FT-17 light tanks. Crews from the 342nd CAC were in Calais during the evacuation and appear to have taken possession of ten abandoned British tanks including several A10s. These were used during operations to protect the evacuation but it seems likely that all were captured by the Germans following the fall of the city.

The losses suffered by 3rd RTR on contact with German tanks were not encouraging. But these new tanks had been used largely in defensive positions and were unable to follow the tactical doctrine of manoeuvre warfare for which they had been designed. It was hoped that the remaining five battalions of the 1st Armoured Division would fare better.

***

The remaining battalions of the 2nd and 3rd Armoured Brigades arrived in Cherbourg in Normandy between 21st and 23rd May. These units were not fully trained or equipped. The intention had been to keep the 1st

Armoured Division in England until it was ready for combat, but the rapid pace of the German advance meant that it was rushed to France before it was combat-ready. For example, the BESA machine guns used in its A10s did not arrive in France until a day or so after the battalions. Many crews had never seen or fired this weapon before and were left to fit and learn how to use these new guns in combat. In general, the A9s and A10s that comprised the bulk of the Cruiser tanks used in France were *"deplorably equipped in comparison to the Germans.*[2]*"*

The A9s and A10s were supplemented by two versions of the A13, but this was a new tank and crews had spent very little time training. Many were sent into combat unfamiliar with the new tank's systems and weapons. There were shortages of optics, radios and even armour-piercing ammunition. Later, the commander of 1st Armoured Division, Major-General Roger Evans, submitted a report noting that this unit was *"a travesty of an armoured division"*[3].

---

[2] Upton P, *The Tenth: 10th Royal Hussars (Prince of Wales' Own) 1715-1969*, BAS Printers Ltd, 1999
[3] Evans R, *General Evans' summary of events*, WO 106/334

Universal Carriers and Vickers Light Tank Mk. VIs of the 4/7th Royal Dragoon Guards in France, early 1940. Most British tanks in France were light tanks.

Image: Imperial War Museum via Wikimedia Commons

Even when they were instructed to embark for France, many personnel assumed that the Armoured Brigades would be given additional time for training and refitting when they arrived in Cherbourg. Instead, War Office orders quickly arrived, instructing the tanks of 1st Armoured Division to immediately move west to secure four key bridgeheads across the Somme held by German forces in and around the town of

Abbeville, 350kms east of Cherbourg. They were then to push north-west to link up with other units of the BEF. For a fully equipped and trained Armoured Division supported by mechanized artillery and infantry, this would have been a challenging mission. For the inadequately equipped and poorly trained 1st Armoured Division, it was, at the very least, a daunting prospect. Major-General Evans noted:

> *"I realised that an operation to secure a crossing over an un-reconnoitred water obstacle, attempted without the artillery and infantry of my support group, and carried out by armoured units arriving piecemeal from detrainment was hazardous and unpromising of success.[4]"*

By this time, 1st Armoured Division had been seconded to the newly created French 10th Army under the command of General Robert Altmayer, Evans protested to Altmayer that his forces were unsuitable for this mission, but he was over-ruled. Altmayer reassured Evans by telling him that French reconnaissance showed that only light defences were present. This was simply untrue. There had been no

---

[4] *Ibid.*

effort to probe the defences and some German units had been in possession of the Somme crossings for five days, giving them ample time to prepare defences that included anti-tank guns.

It was agreed that the assault by 1st Armoured Division would begin early in the morning of 27th May. Altmayer also claimed that the British tanks would be supported by French infantry units. The first engagement involved the 10th Hussars, whose unit diary confidently noted: *"French reconnaissance reports stated that this position was held by inferior troops equipped with only light anti-tank weapons."*

Thirty tanks of the 10th Hussars encountered German anti-tank guns concealed in an orchard near the village of Huppy. They attacked without infantry or artillery support and, within minutes, 20 of the British tanks were destroyed or disabled and the survivors reeled back. Nearby, the 2nd Queen's Bays attacked German positions near the town of Bailleul. Rolling over the crest of a hill, they made perfect targets for concealed German Pak 36 anti-tanks guns. The first four tanks to crest the rise were immediately destroyed. The Bays withdrew and then launched another attack. Once again they were driven back, losing 12 tanks in to the German guns.

The 2nd RTR were able to reach the hamlet of Miannay. No German forces were sighted, but the promised French infantry support had not materialised and, unwilling to enter the small town without infantry, the unit withdrew. 5th RTR was able to occupy the strategically vital heights above the town of St. Valery. Once again, the promised French infantry support was absent, and the tanks were unable to make an attack on the town.

When it arrived in France on 22nd May, 1st Armoured Division brought with it over 270 tanks including more than 150 Cruisers. By the end of 27th May, only 65 Cruisers and 64 Light Tanks remained operational. By 7th June, although it had not taken part in large-scale operations in the meantime, 1st Armoured Division had a total of just 78 serviceable tanks remaining.

By 17th June, 3rd Brigade had retreated to Cherbourg. During the night of 17/18th June, over 30,000 men and 26 tanks were evacuated from the port and returned to England. 2nd Brigade evacuated from Brest, but was forced to abandon all its tanks.

Two A10 Mk. IIAs lead a Valentine and two Matilda IIs at the Central Ordnance Depot at Chilwell, Nottinghamshire, in August 1940.

Image: Imperial War Museum via Wikimedia Commons

The campaign in France was an unmitigated disaster for 1st Armoured Division. It lasted less than four weeks and the new Cruiser tanks were unready for battle and crews were inadequately trained. The Division was used in operations for which it was fundamentally unsuited. Assaulting prepared positions was a mission for infantry tanks, not the lightly armoured Cruisers and they proved very vulnerable when faced with German anti-tanks guns.

The British doctrine of using large unsupported formations of tanks proved to be ineffective when faced with German formations that included anti-tank guns and supporting infantry. A later wartime report on German tactics noted that:

> *"Small antitank units such as the platoon and company are organic parts of larger organizations (regiments and battalions), and their mission is to provide these organizations with defense from armored attack.*
>
> *The antitank battalion of an armored division goes into the attack with the tanks, following them from objective to objective, and engages all tanks threatening them from the flanks and rear.*[5]*"*

These integrated tactics, combining tanks and anti-tank units, proved lethal to unsupported tanks such as the lightly armoured A9s and A10s. Worst of all, the A9s and A10s had proved to be extremely unreliable in combat. More of these tanks were lost to mechanical failures than to enemy action. The main issue was a tendency to throw tracks, which were

---

[5] *German Antitank Units and Tactics*, Tactical and Technical Trends, U.S. War Department, October 1942.

complex and difficult to replace. In peacetime, this wasn't a particular problem. Given time, tracks could be replaced by the crews or maintenance personnel. In combat, losing a track often meant that a tank had to be abandoned.

The AEC engines also proved underpowered and liable to overheating as were the brakes, which limited the tank's manoeuvrability. The armour, especially that fitted to the A9, was inadequate. The armour on the A9 could be penetrated even by the 20mm main gun on the Panzer II and the complex arrangement of machine gun turrets and the central driver's armoured box provided lethal shot-traps that channelled frontal shots. Even the more heavily armoured A10 was vulnerable to both the Pak 36 anti-tank gun and the 37mm main gun on the Panzer III.

The QF 2-Pdr., previously considered an effective weapon, was found wanting in combat. It was capable in an anti-armour role, but when confronted by anti-tank guns in prepared positions, the lack of an effective HE round limited its ability. The A10 in particular was too slow for the Cruiser role, especially when compared to the new A13s coming in to service. Both the A9 and A10 had crew access hatches that were rather small, making getting out of a damaged or burning tank dangerously difficult.

The loss of so many tanks in France left Britain critically short and the remaining A9s and A10s as well as those still in production would be retained in service despite their obvious shortcomings. Winston Churchill personally ordered the highest possible production of existing tank designs in 1940. Britain produced over 1,300 tanks in 1940, more than Germany, but many were the A9s and A10s that had proved ineffective in France.

Even the Germans seemed to agree that these early British Cruisers were not useful tanks. Following the fall of France, the Germans captured a lot of French and British tanks. Many of the French tanks were subsequently modified and taken into German service including the SOMUA S-35, Char B1 bis, Hotchkiss H-35/H-39 and the Renault R-35. Even the diminutive Tracteur Blindé 37L (Lorraine) artillery tractor was repurposed as the basis for the first generation of Marder self-propelled anti-tank guns.

A captured A10 in German markings, though none were used operationally in German service.

Deutsches Bundesarchiv via Wikimedia Commons

More than 20 A9s and A10s were captured more or less intact in France and these were given the German designations of, respectively, *Kreuzer Panzerkampfwagen Mk I 741(e)* and *Kreuzer Panzerkampfwagen Mk II 742(e)*. None were used operationally by the Wehrmacht, even as training tanks, though at least one appears to have been sent to the Kummersdorf proving grounds for evaluation.

The very last attempt to use an A10 in combat took place in 1945 when, in a desperate attempt to stop the Russian advance on Berlin in May 1945, the Cruiser tank sent to Kummersdorf was crewed and sent into combat. As in so many other cases, the A10 broke down before it even reached the front and was abandoned without engaging Russian units.

North Africa

Both A9s and A10s were shipped to North Africa to join 7th Armoured Division, as were both models of the new A13. The A9s and A10s were modified in the field with a two-stage sand filter for the engines and modifications to the cooling system. Some also seem to have been fitted with sand skirts, though most were left as standard. To increase range, some of these tanks were also fitted with additional 35-gallon fuel tanks mounted on the left rear track-guard. These certainly increased range, but were very vulnerable to enemy fire in combat. The problem with overheating brakes which plagued these tanks in France was never completely cured and proved a problem during service in North Africa. One officer familiar with the A9 noted:

> *"The main fault of these tanks, and of the A-10, which gradually replaced them, was that their transmissions and tracks were unreliable. The tracks themselves, and particularly the pins joining the track-plates, were also not robust enough for the hard, stony ground normally met in the desert. It entailed hard work and not a little expert knowledge to keep these*

tanks running for months on end and over long distances.[6]

In this theatre and for the first time, Cruiser tanks were finally used for the role for which they had been designed: rapid manoeuvre warfare.

An A9 crew set up camp near the Libyan border, July 1940.

Image: Imperial War Museum via Wikimedia Commons

By June 1940, all four tank battalions in the 7th Armoured Division had sufficient Cruiser tanks to equip at least one squadron. In September 1940, 2nd RTR joined 7th Armoured Division and brought with it

---

[6] Cyril Joly, *Take These Men*, Penguin Books, 1957,

A9, A10 and A13 Cruisers. The bulk of the early Cruisers used in North Africa were A10 Mark IIAs. Some A9s were used in this theatre, but they were generally replaced by the A10 and A13 as soon as possible.

As early as July 1940, Mussolini had assured Hitler that Italian forces were about to mount an invasion of British-controlled Egypt. The Italian commander, Maresciallo (Marshal) Rodolfo Graziani, was extremely cautious and spent time attempting to build up his forces, particularly dealing with a shortage of transport. In September, Graziani was issued an ultimatum by Mussolini: attack immediately or be replaced. Reluctantly, Graziani ordered his forces to move east into Egypt. This was the first in a series of engagements in North Africa in a campaign that would last until May 1943.

A10s were used in combat for the first time in North Africa on 16th November 1940 when B Squadron, 6th RTR, equipped with 5 A10s and 5 Light tanks, took part in an action to re-take Gallabat fort in Sudan which had been occupied by Italian forces. The fort was re-taken successfully, but all the A10s broke their tracks on the rocky ground.

The main Italian advance into Egypt, *Operazione E*, did not push far into British territory. After just three days and an advance of less than sixty miles, the Italians stopped, dug-in and created defensive position at three camps at Maktila, Tummar and East Tummar West and two more camps on the escarpment to the south-west at Nibeiwa and Sofafi. Operation Compass, the first large-scale British operation in North Africa began in December 1940. At first, this was planned as a short, five-day raid to drive the Italians back to the Libyan border, but it succeeded beyond the wildest dreams of British commanders.

Operation Compass began on the night of 7/8th December. Matilda II infantry tanks of 7th RTR, supported by an Indian Infantry Brigade, attacked the camp at Nibeiwa. When this was taken, this group moved on to successfully assault the camps at Tummar and East Tummar West. The heavily armoured Matilda II proved to be able to shrug off fire from Italian anti-tank weapons. Initially, the Cruisers of 7th Armoured Division were used to protect the flanks of 7th RTR but, when the camps were taken, the Cruisers were finally allowed to do what they had been designed for: to advance rapidly across the open desert towards Libya.

The Cruisers of the 7th Armoured Division were used to pursue the retreating Italian forces on the coast. They met Italian tanks, mainly light tankettes and M11/39s and were able to defeat them without difficulty. The 2-Pdr. guns of the cruisers proved lethal to the lightly armoured Italian tanks and the poor training of Italian crews meant that these tanks were seldom used effectively. The main impediment to the British advance was the sheer number of prisoners taken. By 15th December, British forces had driven Italian forces out of Egypt and had taken more than 30,000 Italian prisoners and captured more than 70 tanks in addition to destroying many more. British casualties were less than five hundred killed and wounded. A number of British tanks were out of action, but most were due to mechanical failures rather than enemy action.

In January, the British moved into Libya and the Cruisers of the 3rd and 7th Hussars and 2nd RTR were used to pursue the retreating Italians. For the first time, the British encountered the new M13/40 medium tanks, but these too were defeated without major losses. The British advance finally ran out of steam in late January, partly due to mechanical failures amongst the tanks of 7th Armoured Division. The attack was called off on 9th February, by which time British forces had taken the provinces of eastern Libya including the port of Tobruk and had captured 25,000 more Italian prisoners and more than 100 additional tanks.

Operation Compass was a massive and largely unexpected success. The Italian 10th Army lost in total at least 5,000 men killed, 10,000 wounded and over 130,000 taken prisoner. More than 400 Italian tanks were destroyed or captured. This operation also seemed to vindicate the concept of manoeuvre warfare by large armoured forces, the role for which the Cruisers had been intended. When fighting against Italian M11/39 and M13/40 Medium tanks, the Cruiser tanks and crews of 7th Armoured Division had proved themselves superior.

By the time that the operation ended, the A9 and A10 tanks used had covered over 500 miles in just ten weeks most were completely worn out and in need of urgent refurbishment. Unlike the campaign in France, the Cruisers were not generally put out of action by adversity or enemy action, but by the sheer scale and scope of their unexpected success.

An A9 being taken for repair on a Scammel tank transporter.

Image: Imperial War Museum via Wikimedia Commons

Both A9s and A10s were particularly badly affected with engines, clutches, suspension and tracks all falling prey to travel over long distances and on rough desert terrain. A shortage of spares and the fact that many tanks were far from their bases meant that these problems were very difficult to address.

By early February 1941, many units of the 7th Armoured Division were combat-ineffective, though personnel were jubilant about their victories. Most of the remaining tanks of 7th Armoured Division were withdrawn to the Nile Delta for refitting and British and Commonwealth forces were deployed in defensive positions in Libya. Although no-one knew it at the time, this was the last easy victory against Italian forces. Soon, German units would arrive in North Africa and the elation of Operation Compass would quickly become no more than a distant memory.

The other reason for calling off Operation Compass in early February was a shift in focus. Winston Churchill was concerned about the possibility of a German attack in the Balkans and on Greece. Part of 7th Armoured Division and some of the infantry units that took part in Operation Compass as well as much of the air support was to be transferred to Greece.

On 11th January 1941, even as British forces were advancing into Libya, Hitler had authorized the formation of a German expeditionary force to support his Italian allies in North Africa, the Deutsches Afrika

Korps (DAK). On 11th February, General Erwin Rommel, who had effectively commanded 7th Panzer Division in France, was appointed to lead the new force.

Two A9s near Tobruk in 1941.

Image: Imperial War Museum via Wikimedia Commons

The purpose of the DAK was simply to prevent further British advances in Libya. As Panzer II, III and IV tanks began to arrive in Libya, Rommel quickly decided instead to conduct an *"armoured reconnaissance,"* as he had been forbidden from mounting an attack. This soon became a full-scale offensive, driving the British back to Tobruk and beyond. By April, German and Italian forces had advanced into Egypt and taken the town of Sollum and the tactically important Halfaya Pass.

On 15th June, the British launched Operation Battleaxe, an attempt to relieve Tobruk and drive the Germans back. 2nd RTR, mainly equipped with A9s and A10s was used to lead the assault on a series of ridges at Hafid. As the Cruisers crested the first ridge, they were engaged by German anti-tank guns and two were immediately destroyed. The Cruisers withdrew, and then tried a different approach, moving to the western edge of the ridges and turning into the first valley. The commander spotted a fortified position ahead and called off the attack. Five of the Cruisers (which did not have radios) continued and all were quickly destroyed by more German anti-tank guns.

It then appeared that the Germans were retreating and 6th RTR, who were following behind, were sent to pursue in their new A15 Crusader tanks. It was a trap and the Crusaders ran into yet another concealed

German anti-tank line. Within a few minutes, eleven of the attacking Crusaders were destroyed and six more badly damaged. By the end of this first day of the operation, 2nd RTR was reduced to just 28 Cruisers and 6th RTR had lost 30 of the 50 Crusaders with which it had started the day.

The following day, the British encountered German tanks, mainly Panzer IVs and the new Panzer III Ausf. F equipped with the powerful 5 cm KwK 38 L/42 gun. The German tanks units used devastatingly effective tactics. The Panzer IVs fired HE rounds from their 75mm guns from beyond the range of the British tank's 2-Pdr guns. These rounds forced the British artillery support to withdraw. With the artillery removed, the Panzer IIIs would then attack using their 50mm guns, also from beyond the range of the 2-Pdrs. These guns were capable penetrating the armour on all British Cruisers, but the A9s and A10s were especially vulnerable. If the British tanks advanced to close the range so that they could return fire, they would be drawn on to a screen of concealed anti-tanks guns. By evening, only 21 Cruisers remained operational.

In the three days of Operation Battleaxe, the British lost over 90 tanks, including 30 cruisers and 65 Matilda IIs. Virtually no ground was re-taken and the siege of Tobruk continued. In November, the British launched another major attack named Operation Crusader. This would be the last operation in North Africa that included A10 Cruiser tanks (no A9s then remained in front-line service).

Most British tank units had received improved Cruiser tanks, including large numbers of the A15 Crusader (after which the operations was named), and the M3 Stuart light tank. Only two units of 7th Armoured Division were still using A10s, the HQ Section of 7th Armoured Brigade and the 7th Hussars. By the time of Operation Crusader, the A10 had become something of a liability. Its armour was relatively thin, its 2-Pdr gun was out-ranged by the 50mm gun in the upgraded Panzer III and its lack of speed compared to other Cruiser tanks made it difficult for mixed units to operate cohesively.

The main focus of Operation Crusader was the port of Tobruk. The Afrika Korps was hampered by long supply lines stretching back into Libya and Rommel wanted to occupy Tobruk. The British wanted to relieve the siege of the city so that they could use the port to provide supplies to units pushing into Libya. 7th Armoured Division was given the task of pushing ahead towards Tobruk. Overall, British forces enjoyed a notable advantage in tank numbers, with over seven hundred facing around 250 German and 150 Italian tanks.

The British attack began on 18th November and, initially made good progress. The critical moment for 7th Armoured Brigade came on November 21st/22nd when 2nd and 6th RTR and the 7th Hussars faced German panzers close to the airfield at Sidi Rezegh. 6th RTR were left to guard the airfield while 2nd RTR and the 7th Hussars moved to engage the German tanks of the 21st Panzer Division. In two days of confused and fluctuating fighting, 7th Armoured Brigade lost 113 of the141 tanks with which it began this engagement. The only surviving tanks in 7th Hussars were 10 A10s, but these were critically short of fuel and took no further part in Operation Crusader.

The operational report produced by the commander of the 7th Hussars after the battle at Sidi Rezegh made several important points:

"In the initial stages the enemy appeared to move his tank force in a concentrated mass. The column which attacked 7th Hussars on November 21st was a densely packed tank force numbering some 150 tanks.

The enemy opened fire at long range and several tanks of the 7th Hussars were destroyed before they could close to effective 2 – pounder range.

Tanks of a Regiment should be all of the same type. 7th Hussars went into action with a mixture of A 15, A 13, and A 10 Cruiser tanks."

The 2-Pdr, which had been a marginally effective weapon in 1940, was simply outclassed by German guns in 1941. Trying to operate units that included faster and more recent Cruisers alongside the now elderly A10s simply slowed formations to the speed of the slowest tanks or led to uncoordinated attacks. A belated recognition of the facts led to the withdrawal of the last A10s from front-line service and the production of a new version of the A15 Crusader armed with the more powerful 6-Pdr. gun.

Operation Crusader succeeded in relieving the siege of Tobruk, but at a high cost to the British. Tank losses amounted to 530 in total compared to just 100 German tanks destroyed. The Afrika Korps was forced to temporarily retreat, but in January 1942, launched a counter-attack which saw British forces driven back to Gazala.

When A9s and A10s first arrived in North Africa, they performed well in rapid manoeuvre warfare against Italian forces. When they were used against improved German tanks, they proved extremely vulnerable and their reliability was always suspect. Although a few A10s remained in service in several locations including Malta and Cyprus, these early Cruisers never saw combat again after November 1941.

Greece

In March 1941, a contingent of British and Commonwealth forces were sent to Greece to help the Greek Army counter the German invasion. Two armoured units were included: 4th Hussars equipped with 53 Mark VI light tanks and 3rd RTR, equipped with 52 battle-weary A10s. 3rd RTR had been provided with two Squadrons of A13s, but had been forced to exchange these for A10s before leaving Egypt.

The experienced crews of 3rd RTR were under no illusions about the effectiveness of their A10s. While the tanks and crew were being transported to Greece by sea, one officer recalled that:

> *"We discussed with our naval hosts the inadequacies of our tanks, describing with affectionate abuse the thin armour, the ridiculous 2 pdr gun and the inability of the whole outfit to move more than a few miles in heavy going without shedding a track.[7]"*

These units would face 5 German Divisions including the 2nd and 9th Panzer Divisions. 3rd RTR arrived in

---

[7] Robert Crisp, *The Gods Were Neutral*, W.W. Norton, 1961

Piraeus and set up camp outside Athens on 11th March. The unit was required to move to the north of Greece and, to save the risk of breakdowns, the A10s were transported by rail to the town of Florina in north-western Macedonia, around 30km from the Yugoslavian border.

The German invasion began on 6th April and it rapidly became clear that the combined British and Greek forces lacked the equipment and numbers to stop the German advance. They began a long retreat, bombed continually by German aircraft. The tanks of 3rd RTR were able to engage German light armour from prepared ambush sites as they withdrew and a number of Panzer IIs and armoured cars were destroyed. Although they were able to slow the German advance, 3rd RTR could not stop it and in each engagement, they lost tanks to German guns as well as to numerous breakdowns.

The rugged terrain of northern Greece proved lethal to the fragile tracks, suspension and engines of the A10s. A lack of spares made these problems even more serious. When spare parts did arrive, it was discovered that they were for A13 and A15 Cruisers, not for the A10s that 3rd RTR were using!

A10s of 3rd RTR abandoned in Greece.

Image: Deutsches Bundesarchiv via Wikimedia Commons

A confidential report issued after the Greek campaign listed no fewer than 16 A10s lost to breakdowns, including 11 to broken tracks. Some sources suggest that only 6 A10s were lost to enemy action in Greece, with all the rest being abandoned due to breakdowns.

By 15th April, 3rd RTR was reduced to just 12 serviceable tanks. By the 18th, after less than two weeks of combat, all the unit's tanks had been knocked out or had broken down. No replacements were available and the 3rd RTR ceased to be an effective fighting force.

Another A10 of 3rd RTR, abandoned after breaking a track. Virtually all the wartime photographs of A10s in Greece are German images of abandoned tanks.

Image: Deutsches Bundesarchiv via Wikimedia Commons

On the 27th April, the surviving personnel of 3rd RTR were evacuated as part of a larger operation that saw the evacuation of all British forces from Greece. For all the bravery of its men, the loss of all its Cruiser tanks and many casualties, 3rd RTR had been unable to materially affect the German occupation of Greece.

Colour Schemes and Markings

Colour Schemes

This is a brief overview of the colour schemes and markings used on A9 and A10 tanks. It is by no means a comprehensive guide to this subject, something that might well fill a whole book on its own. If you would like to find more detailed information, the *Further Reading* section includes a guide to suitable publications.

The A9 and A10 were only used by units of the British Army. Most colours used on these tanks were specified by using British Standards. The concept of standardised specifications for a whole range of items began with the Engineering Standards Committee in 1901. In 1929 this group received a Royal Charter and, in 1931, became the British Standards Institute, the name under which it continues to operate to the present day. The work of the BSI was supplemented by the British Colour Council (BCC), founded in 1931. This group produced the first comprehensive British standardised colour reference in the *British Colour Council reference Code* which identified a range of colours through a two or three-digit code and a name.

The colours were identified through the production of printed plates and many were adopted in British Standards such as B.S.381C: of 1930, *Colours for Ready-Mixed Paints.* Some of the colours were specifically intended for the armed forces, such as *Battleship Grey* CC 322, *Rifle Green* CC 264 and *Scarlet Red* CC 22.

Colours were matched by comparing them to the samples provided by the BCC and there was no attempt to define colours by using, for example, the RAL colour standard defined in Germany in the 1920s. All the samples produced in the 1930s have faded and deteriorated over time, and this makes it very difficult to precisely match these colours today. Another problem was that the chromate compounds used for paints in the 1930s were unstable and could change colour with exposure to light or even through contact with air. So even samples taken from vehicles of the period in locations where they are protected from light may have changed colour over time.

This makes it problematic for anyone seeking to restore a British vehicle from the 1930s to confidently match the original colour. The challenge is even greater for scale modellers due to the scale colour effect. This is a visual phenomenon where distance affects the perception of colour. This means that, even if you are able to precisely match the colour of a real vehicle, if you use this colour on a small-scale model, it will look too dark. In effect, looking at a 1/72 model from three feet away is the equivalent of viewing the original from over 200 feet, at which distance the scale colour effect will make the vehicle's colour seem lighter. Viewing a 1/35 model from three feet away is the equivalent of viewing the original from 100 feet, at which distance the scale colour effect will still affect perception of colour, but to a lesser extent. There is general acceptance that the scale colour effect is a real phenomenon, but no agreement on how much colours should be lightened to suit various scales.

Finally, there are wartime photographs of the vehicles involved. The colours used in many camouflage schemes, while clearly evident to the eye, have relatively low contrast. Using 1930s black and white film, and depending on lighting conditions and the camera involved, the colours used can be indistinguishable, making camouflaged tanks and other vehicles appear to be painted in a single uniform colour. All of which means that precise definitions of colours used on wartime vehicles are difficult to achieve, and perhaps are better taken as a general guide rather than a detailed specification.

France

The British Army in the 1930s defined vehicle paint schemes through Military Training Pamphlets (MTPs) and Army Council Instructions (ACIs) which established colours using B.S. 391C and provided guidance on the application of camouflage schemes. Paint was supplied Prepared for Use (PFU), i.e., pre-mixed to match BSI standards. The schemes used on A9 and A10 tanks of the BEF in France were defined in *Military Training Pamphlet No. 20 Camouflage: disruptive painting of vehicles*, issued in June 1939.

The standard camouflage pattern is clearly visible in this photograph of an A10 abandoned in France.

Image: Deutsches Bundesarchiv via Wikimedia Commons

On these tanks (as on all other British tanks of the period), the base colour was Khaki Green G3 with a disruptive, hard-edged camouflage pattern of Dark Green No.4. From May 1940, the camouflage colour was changed to Dark Tarmac No.4 as stocks of the original dark green ran low. The majority of A9s and A10s used in France were supplied before this change and most would have had the original Khaki Green G3/ Dark Green No.4 scheme.

The Middle East

For vehicles used in North Africa, the situation was different. Colours and schemes for vehicles in that theatre were defined through Middle East General Orders (MEGO). Most tanks arrived in the Middle East from the middle of 1940 onwards painted in the new standard Khaki Green G3/Dark Tarmac No.4 scheme. These were then overpainted with new schemes when they arrived in the Middle East.

MEGO 370, issued in July 1939, specified a base colour of Middle Stone No. 62 with a hard-edged disruptive camouflage pattern in Dark Sand in the same pattern specified in MTP 20. However, photographs seem to show that many vehicles, including Cruiser tanks, were initially painted only in the base colour of Middle Stone No. 62. Later, by the middle of 1940, the disruptive camouflage pattern of Dark Sand seems to have been added to most tanks.

In November 1940, MEGO 297 specified a new, three-colour scheme to be used on all AFVs. This scheme is generally referred to as the *"Caunter Scheme,"* named after the officer who created it. This comprised bold stripes of Light Stone 61, Silver Grey 28 and Khaki

Green G3, though other combinations of colour were used depending on the availability of paint.

An A10 painted in the Caunter Scheme in North Africa.

Image: Imperial War Museum via Wikimedia Commons

Shortages of paint led to the introduction of a two-colour version of this scheme, known as the *"Sudan Scheme."* This used stripes of Light Stone No.61 and Light Purple Brown No. 49.

From October 1941, by which time most A9s and A10s had been withdrawn from front-line service, continuing shortages of paint meant that a new scheme in overall Light Stone 61 was introduced for all British tanks in the Middle East.

Greece

The colours used on British A10s sent to Greece with 3rd RTR is a matter of some debate. These tanks were sent from the Middle East, and it is generally assumed that they retained the camouflage they received in that theatre when they were transferred to Greece. Anecdotal evidence suggests that this view may be mistaken. At least one personal account by a young Australian artillery officer involved in the Greek campaign noted:

> *"The Greek Air Force had recamouflaged our guns and vehicles, changing the colour scheme from the slate, white and grey of the desert to green and brown.[8]"*

It is not known if this re-painting was also done to A10s and whether the colours used were those normally used by the British Army or by the Greek Air Force. Other sources suggest that the tanks of 3rd RTR sent to Greece were painted before leaving Egypt in a base of Light Stone No.61 with a camouflage pattern in some unknown additional colour.

---

[8] Michael Clarke, *My War 1939 – 1945*, Michael Clarke Press, 1990.

This 3rd RTR A10 Mk. IIA CS abandoned in Greece clearly has an unusual camouflage scheme, but it is impossible to ascertain from this black and white image just what colours were used.

Image: Deutsches Bundesarchiv via Wikimedia Commons

Markings

Unlike virtually every other major combatant nation in World War Two, British tanks and other military vehicles carried no national markings. The closest to this was the Royal Tank Corps white/red/white flash carried on many British early-war tanks. This was not universally used and this marking is not found in any wartime photograph of an A9 or A10. The RTC flash was added to tanks in North Africa from late 1941, but by that time most of the early Cruisers had been withdrawn from front-line service. However, British tanks carried a number of other markings.

All British tanks carried a War Department census number, usually in white for European colour schemes and in black for tanks in North Africa. This was assigned during manufacture and was unique to a particular tank and comprised the letter "T" (for "tracked vehicle") followed by four to seven digits. On A9s and A10s, these 3½" high stencilled numbers were generally placed on the edge of the track-guards on either side, on the lower front hull and on the rear hull. Placement varied, with some tanks only having this number on front and rear, and on photographs of some tanks in North Africa, this number seems to have been left off altogether.

In the pre-war and very early war period, tanks were also assigned registration numbers, just like other non-military road vehicles. These were displayed on standard black number plates with white characters fixed to the hull front and rear. The practise of assigning tanks registration numbers was dropped in 1939. So, for example, the first batch of 50 A9s produced at the Elswick works was assigned registration numbers from HMH848 - HMH897. The second batch of A9s produced at Harland & Wolff was not assigned registration numbers. Where tanks were fitted with a registration number plate, the War Department census number was painted in smaller digits next to the plate. The 3½" tall census numbers were used on tanks not assigned a registration number, generally anything produced from early 1940 on.

Most British tanks also carried a marking identifying the division to which they were attached. For example, tanks of the 1st Armoured Division in France carried that division's white rhinoceros marking on the front hull while tanks of the 7th Armoured Division in North

Africa carried that division's red and white jerboa (desert rat) marking.

Most British Regiments were divided into more than one battalion. Battalions were often assigned to different divisions, and it was rare for two battalions from the same regiment to fight together. Battalion (Arm of Service) markings on tanks generally took the form of a 9" square, red for the HQ battalion and green for the three line battalions. White numbers inside these squares denoted battalions with "8" for the senior, "9" for the next senior and "10" for the junior.

Armoured Divisions comprised three Armoured Brigades, each comprising three battalions. The three battalions assigned to each Brigade were further divided into four squadrons (sometimes referred to as "*troops*" in cavalry regiments), each consisting of three tanks.

Each battalion within a Brigade was also assigned colours, with red used for the senior regiment, yellow for the next most senior and blue for the least senior. Seniority was assigned according to a complex and arcane order of precedence. Generally, this was based on the date upon which the battalion first entered service, though certain battalions such as Guards Regiments were automatically given a higher seniority. For RTR battalions, seniority was assigned purely on the basis of the battalion number, with 1st RTR being the most senior.

This A9 CS of 3rd RTR abandoned in Calais in 1940 after breaking a track carries the 1st Armoured Division marking (a white rhinoceros) on the upper front hull, the bridge weight limit marking ("13" inside a yellow circle) and an arm-of service marking on the lower front hull. It also has a triangular tactical marking on the front and rear side of the turret.

Image: Deutsches Bundesarchiv Bild 146-1971-042-10

Tanks carried tactical markings, generally on their turrets, using these colours plus shapes to denote squadrons within battalions. Thus, HQ Squadron tanks carried a diamond, A Squadron a triangle, B Squadron a square and C Squadron a circle. So, for example a tank with a red triangle on its turret would belong to A Squadron of the most senior battalion within the division.

Where tanks were given names by their crews, these generally used the Squadron letter, so tanks in C Squadron would have names beginning with the letter "C", for example, though this practice was not universally followed.

British tanks in World War Two also generally carried a Bridge Rating marking, a 7½" yellow circle with black numerals painted on the lower front hull. The number carried within the plate was the bridge category, based on the tank's overall weight rounded up to the next ton: "13" for the A9 and "15" for the A10. Many wartime photographs seem to show A9s and A10s without this marking.

Surviving Examples

Only two A9s and a single A10 survive today. Two of these tanks are in the Tank Museum at Bovington in Dorset on the southern coast of England. Bovington has been a military camp since the land was purchased for a firing range in 1899. It wasn't until author Rudyard Kipling visited the camp in the 1920s that anyone considered preserving tanks here. Kipling saw the rusting hulks of several British tanks from World War One and suggested that they should be preserved. From virtually that time on, examples of tanks no longer needed in British service have been sent to the museum and preserved. Captured tanks, once they have been tested and evaluated, have also been sent to Bovington. The museum opened to the public in 1947 and now has a collection of over 300 tanks.

The A9 at The Tank Museum is T7230, built at Harland and Wolff in February 1940. This particular A9 never saw active service during World War Two, being sent from the factory to the School of Tank technology before being passed to The Tank Museum. This tank has been restored in the colours and markings used by A9s of the 3rd RTR, 1st Armoured Division used in France.

T7230, the A9 Cruiser Mk. I on display at the Tank Museum, Bovington. The White rhinoceros on the front hull is the insignia of 1st Armoured Division.

Image: Simon via Wikimedia Commons

The A10 at the Tank Museum is T9261, built by the Metropolitan Cammell Carriage and Wagon Company. This is an A10 Mark IIA CS, armed with two BESA machine guns and a 3.7inch howitzer in the turret. This tank was used by A Squadron, 5th Royal Tank Regiment and it is also preserved in the colours and markings of an A10 of the 1st Armoured Division in France.

T9261, the A10 Cruiser Mk. II CS on display at the Tank Museum, Bovington.

Image: Makizox via Wikimedia Commons

The only other surviving A9 is on display at the Armoured Corps Museum in Ahmednagar, Maharashtra, India. This is an original A9 armed with three Vickers water-cooled machine guns. The tank is finished in overall khaki green and carries virtually no markings or other identification. The lockers on the upper hull are missing, it appears to have been fitted with non-standard tracks and the main gun barrel has been replaced with a long section of steel tube.

This is Asia's only tank museum and has on display a range of British and other tanks ranging from WW1 to the 1960s. The museum is operated by the adjacent Armored Corps Centre and School and has around 50 exhibits in total.

The A9 Cruiser Mk. I on display at the Armoured Corps Museum in Ahmednagar, Maharashtra, India.

Image: Mohit S via Wikimedia Commons

One other A10 is currently undergoing restoration by a small private group based in Lincolnshire, England. The group, led by Carl Brown and Adrian Barrel, recovered the battered remains of the hull of an A10 from an Army firing range in the early 2000s and the group plans to restore the tank to running condition: a mammoth task! It is believed that this may be the original A10E1 prototype supplied to the army in 1937. When restored, this will be the only 2-Pdr. armed A10 in existence. You can follow the progress of the restoration on the group's Facebook page at:

https://www.facebook.com/cruisermk2/

Conclusion

The A10 and the A9 from which it was derived were seriously flawed designs. The utility of the multi-turret design of the A9 was dubious and on many examples, the machine gun turret gunners were dispensed with and the space used instead to stow additional ammunition. The A10 was neither sufficiently heavily armoured to offer protection against German anti-tank guns nor fast enough to take on the Cruiser role effectively. Problems with engine and brake overheating noted on the prototypes of both types were never fully addressed. The rate of thrown and broken tracks was little short of a scandal, exemplified by the Greek campaign that may have seen up to 75% of all the A10s of 3rd RTR put out of action by track-related breakdowns.

Many of these problems were due to cost-cutting in the design and a need to re-use existing technology and components on the new Cruisers. The desire for a *"reasonably cheap tank"* is simply not compatible with an operational need for a reasonably effective and reliable tank. With hindsight, the desire to rush these tanks into production is perhaps understandable. War was coming. Britain had a new armoured tactical doctrine that seemed to be the only way to counter the threat of German aggression in Europe. But it had no tanks capable of executing this new doctrine. Britain needed Cruiser tanks and it needed them quickly.

The refusal to systematically implement improvements is less understandable. The shortcomings in the A9 were evident in the first prototype delivered in April 1936. The first production models were not delivered to the British Army until almost three years later, in early 1939. The first versions of the German Panzer III had similar problems in 1936, but in the space of two years it was improved and refined to become a reliable and effective tank. In contrast, no significant improvements were made to the basic design of the A9 and production versions differed only in detail from the prototype. Germany manufactured prototype tanks and used these to understand what needed to be improved for production versions. Britain seems to have been content simply to manufacture prototypes in large numbers.

The British Army went to war in September 1939 with a Cruiser Tank based on an outdated design concept that was also unreliable and provided with inadequate armour. These problems were known and understood in 1936, but the fact that nothing was done to address these before they were sent into combat in 1940 is perhaps the most baffling and disappointing aspect of the story of both the A9 and A10.

This might be more understandable if the next generation of British Cruisers, coming into service as the war had begun, had used the experience of designing the A9 and A10 to provide notably better tanks. Instead, the subsequent A13 and A15 simply introduced new problems and exposed new weaknesses. Britain would not finally produce an effective Cruiser tank that combined adequate mobility, firepower and protection until the A34 Comet introduced late in 1944. Up to then, too many British tank crews would die or become prisoners or casualties because they were sent into battle in poorly designed tanks of dubious reliability.

World War Two saw quantum leaps in tank design and the appearance of some highly innovative and effective tanks. Sadly, almost none of them were British.

Further Reading

Campaign Histories

Blitzkrieg: From the Rise of Hitler to the Fall of Dunkirk, by Len Deighton, Jonathan Cape, 1979. Novelist Deighton is a consummate story-teller. He is also a keen amateur historian with a comprehensive understanding of war from the viewpoints of politics and military technology. In this non-fiction work he uses all these abilities, including the wry humour that characterises his fiction writing, to tell the story not just of how the German attack on the West in May/June 1945 unfolded, but of the wider circumstances that made German victory possible.

To Lose a Battle: France 1940, by Alistair Horne, 1969. More than fifty years after it was first published this remains the definitive account of the German invasion of the west in May 1940. This work not only takes a detailed look at the political developments that led to the attack but also provides an exhaustive review of the battle itself. If you want to understand the fighting in Belgium and France in 1940, this is an indispensable work.

The BEF in France 1939-1940: Manning the Front Through to the Dunkirk Evacuation, by John Grehan and Martin Mace, 2014, Pen and Sword, Casemate Publishers. Dispatches from British commanders during the fighting in France in 1940.

Tank Combat in North Africa: The Opening Rounds Operations Sonnenblume, Brevity, Skorpion and Battleaxe, by Thomas L. Jentz, Schiffer Military History, 1998. A detailed account of early tank battles in North Africa, mainly compiled from the accounts of those who participated.

The Defence and Fall of Greece 1940-41, by John Carr, Pen and Sword Military, 2013. A detailed account of combat in Greece from the Italian invasion to the German occupation.

Technical books

British Cruiser Tanks of World War Two, The War Archives, Pat Ware (Editor). An illustrated history of the development and use of British Cruiser tanks during World War Two, though the A9 and A10 are briefly covered in just four pages.

British Tank Markings and Names: The Unit Markings and paint colors of British

armoured fighting vehicles, 1914 – 1945, by B. T. White, Squadron/Signal Publications, 1978. A detailed and comprehensive guide to colour schemes and markings used on British tanks from 1916 – 1945.

British Army Colours Disruptive Camouflage in the United Kingdom, France & NW Europe 1936-45, by Mike Starmer. This short (around 30 pages), self-published book is an invaluable guide to the colours and camouflage patterns used on British Fighting vehicles during World War Two.

Death by Design: British Tank Development in the Second World War, by Peter Beale, The History Press Ltd, 2009. It now seems to be out of print, but if you can track down a copy, this fascinating book looks in detail at the systemic failures in specification, design and manufacture that led to the generally poor quality of British tanks in World War Two.

A view from the turret

Taming the Panzers: 3rd RTR at War, by Patrick Delaforce, Amberly Publishing, 2010. A detailed account of 3rd RTR during World War Two. Includes the campaigns in France Greece and North Africa as well as battles in Normandy following D-Day. Includes references to many contemporary accounts of combat.

The Gods Were Neutral, by Robert Crisp, Norton, 1961. Bob Crisp was a tank commander with 3rd RTR and this is his account of the campaign in Greece and his experiences of the A10. Crisp also wrote another book about his experiences in tanks in World War Two, *Brazen Chariots*. Both are highly recommended for anyone who wants to understand what fighting in unreliable and ineffective tanks was really like.

Other Books in the *Armour at War* Series

The Armour at War Series is a work in progress with new titles being added as they are completed. Here are the next two planned books in the series, completing the story of British Cruiser Tanks:

A Confusion of Cruisers: A13 Cruiser Tank Mk. III, Mk. IV and MK. V Covenanter and A15 Cruiser Tank Mk. VI Crusader.

The story of British Cruiser tanks continues with a plethora of new designs reflecting confusion about just what these tanks were for and a tendency to introduce completely new designs rather than systematically improve what was already available. In the space of less than three years, six entirely new designs were produced. Four of these, the A13 Cruiser Tanks Mk. III and IV, the Mk. V Covenanter (said by some to have been the worst tank ever used by the British Army) and the A15 Cruiser Tank Mk. VI Crusader, went into production and entered service with the British Army. Two others, the A14 *Heavy Cruiser* and the A16 *Battle Cruiser* were abandoned after prototypes were produced and tested.

Spreading resources over so many new designs squandered opportunities and while each of the new Cruisers brought improvements, they also introduced new failings and continued the Cruiser tradition of suspect reliability. The book includes the context and design history of these tanks plus their use in combat.

The Final Cruisers: A24, A27 and A34, Cavalier, Cromwell and Comet.

Lessons learned from the A13 and A15 led to the last generation of British Cruiser tanks. These were notably better than those that had gone before but it wasn't until the last Cruiser, the A34 Comet, introduced in limited numbers in the final months of World War Two, that Britain finally produced a truly effective and reliable Cruiser Tank. This follows the standard *Armour at War* format with the background and design history of these tanks combined with the story of their development and use in combat.

About the Author

I am a professional writer and I have written more than one hundred books, mainly non-fiction works ghost-written for clients around the world.

I am a Scot, I'm married with two grown-up children and I currently live in beautiful Andalusia in southern Spain.

I first became interested in military history and particular armoured warfare through my father, who served in the Scots Guards in World War Two as first a driver and then a gunner in Churchill tanks. He loved the Churchill and thought it a fine tank, though I was aware that most impartial observers seemed to have a less positive view of the Churchill. That difference between how someone who served in a particular tank felt about it versus conventional histories based on a technical analysis was what prompted me to begin writing the *Armour at War* series. The design and development of a particular tank is fascinating, but without some idea of how the men who fought in these vehicles regarded it, that it is only part of the story.

I welcome input from readers. You can email me with comments or suggestions or on: armouratwar@gmail.com.

Printed in Great Britain
by Amazon